Raped Black Male

A Memoir

By
Kenneth Rogers Jr.

Strategic Book Publishing and Rights Co.

Strategic Book Publishing and Rights Co., LLC
USA | Singapore
www.sbpra.com

For information about special discounts for bulk purchases, please contact Strategic Book Publishing and Rights Co., LLC. Special Sales, at bookorder@sbpra.net.

ISBN: 978-1-68181-540-4

<u>Beginnings</u>

We don't develop courage by being happy every day. We develop it by surviving difficult times and challenging adversity.
– Barbara de Angelis

What does it mean to be a male rape survivor?

This is a question I ask myself most mornings before panic sets in. Usually, it's 4:00 a.m. For the most part, I'm rested, and thoughts of the day begin rushing in. This is when the fear takes hold and won't let go. I do what I've been taught. Meditate.

Breathe in deeply through the nose. Exhale out through the mouth.

Inhale.

Exhale.

Inhale.

Exhale.

This reminds my brain that I'm safe, and I'll continue to be safe.

I think to myself, *It's over. She can't get me here.*

At 4:15 a.m., I find my way through the dark, make coffee, adding too much creamer, and continue to the basement, holding my cell phone, mug, and headphones.

The fear is still there, just below the surface of a calm exterior. I breathe and sit on the couch.

Inhale.

Exhale.

Turning on my phone, I flick to the "White Noise" app, insert headphones, and listen to the sound of crashing waves. They remind me of the Virgin Islands, my wife, Sarah, our honeymoon, and happiness.

For fifteen minutes, I close my eyes and meditate. I begin with the image of stairs hovering in the center of a white room. Each step is labeled with a number, and I stand at the top, facing backwards. I begin to slowly count backwards from ten.

Ten

My feet hang off the edge of the top step.

Nine

I step down, and a new number comes into focus.

Eight

My visualized self never looks back.

Seven

I simply step down . . .

Six

. . . to the next step.

Five

And as I move down the steps . . .

Four

. . . so do my eyes.

Three

Until eventually . . .

Two

. . . I am completely . . .

One

. . . calm.

Zero

And my mind is clear.

The entire time, my breathing is shallow. I remind myself each moment that everything will be fine, letting the different images and thoughts surface and float away until the fifteen minutes is over. I'm calm and the day starts.

For me, this is what it means to be a survivor: finding ways to keep breathing.

The words *raped black male* are rarely together in the same sentence. As homicides of black males at the hands of white police officers continue to rise, the words usually strung together by the media are *armed black male, convicted black male, imprisoned black male*, or something very similar. Less likely to be heard about, or even thought to exist, are *loving, affectionate*, or *gay* black males. Occasionally, we may hear the words *sexy* and *talented* used about black actors or sports stars of the NFL and NBA, instead of *educated* and *intelligent*. If words define people, then what do those words say about how we view blacks in our society?

I don't speak for all blacks or men who have been victims of sexual abuse. This is not a book of statistics. These are my thoughts, beliefs, imaginings, and feelings about what it means to me to be black, a father, a teacher, and a survivor of sexual abuse. Books are meant to heal, help, and inform. I hope this book does all three.

RAPED

Anybody can become angry – that is easy, but to be angry with the right person and to the right degree and at the right time and for the right purpose, and in the right way – that is not within everybody's power and is not easy. – Aristotle

Ankles

On my right ankle there is a scar that covers a portion of my heel and outer ankle. I have the scar because, one summer afternoon in 1991, I was stupid. Stupid is a harsh word, I know, but when you're six-years-old, what else can you be besides brain-dead?

Summers meant very few things for my siblings and myself back then. For me and my older sister, they meant waking up around eleven or twelve, watching daytime television until after *The 700 Club* finally came to an end and cartoons began. For my older brother, Daniel, it meant working in the fields, cleaning corn to earn a little spending money and getting blacker than my Uncle Blue on his worst day. These are the only things I can definitely remember about those hazy days, when for weeks I wouldn't see the sun and an oversized T-shirt was all that covered by bony body for 80 percent of the 24-hour day. However, on that summer afternoon we had a plan, or so I was told.

That morning Daniel said, "We're going to go to the Dollar Theatre. Get ready."

For those of you born during *Generation Selfie*, this was a big deal. In those days, there was no high-speed internet, cell phones, DVR, or even DVDs. There was only the theatre, VHS, and cable. When a movie came to the theatre, it would take close to a year before the movie made it to video. And well over two years before it appeared on any sort of HBO or Disney free weekend subscription to tape it from the television. So if you really wanted to see a movie, you paid the full price to see a movie at Landmark (the nice theatre with the comfy seats down the road), you waited a few weeks until it was playing at the Dollar Theatre, or you never saw it.

The Dollar Theatre was located in Westlake Shopping Center, a small strip mall that held a few Chinese restaurants, a JoAnn Fabric, and the two best places for any kid under the age of fifteen: Toys "R" Us and Show Biz (soon to become Chuck E. Cheese's). This small theatre held six screens, only showed movies that had been in theatres for weeks and had now been retired to where the floors were always sticky, the popcorn was stale, but the Cherry Coke was amazing. If we were going to the movies, it was a cause for celebration and preparation.

Now, in the 21st century of Marty McFly, it's easy to plan a cinematic adventure. All you have to do is: A. take out your cell phone, B. turn on your cell phone, C. open the "Fandango" app on your cell phone and let the fun begin. With a tap of an illuminated light on a glass screen, you have access to every movie playing in every theatre in every zip code, from L.A. to New York, today and five months in the future.

Then, back in the 20th century of Zack Morris, it was an ordeal. First, it meant finding change for a newspaper because the newspaper was the cell phone of the past. It contained all the immediate information you would need to survive the day: weather, entertainment, sports, politics, etc. Usually, money for this staple came from the top of the refrigerator. The secret, but not so secret, place my Dad would put leftover change after buying cigarettes and beer. Once the fifty cents, seventy-five cents, or $1.25 for the Journal Star newspaper (different prices for different days of the week) was acquired, it meant walking to the corner and buying the paper from the gas station. With paper in hand, all that was left to do was find the movie section, see what was playing at what time, and begin the revelry.

Simple as pie.

With paper in hand I scanned the times and what was playing while Daniel and my sister got the bikes out of the garage. I don't remember the movies, or what we chose because we never made it. What I do remember is sitting on the back of Daniel's bike as I held his waist and he pedaled while my sister rode her own bike. I remember my brother telling me to hold tight. I remember him telling me to keep my feet sticking out from the tires. And I remember thinking that if I just brushed against the spokes of the tire with my heels, it would make a funny sound and make Daniel a little annoyed. We hadn't gone very far—just past Woodrow Wilson Elementary across the street from our house—when I moved my heels slowly to the spokes of the tire, just enough to feel the vibration of the moving wheel. I heard a loud crunching sound and immediately flipped onto the pavement as Daniel's bike came to an abrupt stop and the tire ate the entirety of my foot of flesh and bone.

This is where reality blends with fantasy.

In my stupid six-year-old imagination, I lay on my back and hovered above my dying body as the scene played out around me. I watched as my sister threw her bike to the ground in slow motion and scream in terror as Daniel lifted the bike above his head and threw the behemoth down the vacant side street with a sprinkling of sparks. They took one look at the blood dripping from the open wound of my ankle and knew they had to call an ambulance. Eventually, I passed out as my sister cried and Daniel ran to the nearest house to use their phone. I woke up on a hospital bed, watching as a doctor cut away layers of dead skin from my battered and mangled foot with tweezers and a pair of scissors, before applying an ointment that stained my skin a dull maroon. My sister and Daniel stood on either side as the doctor worked, each worried for my life. My sister held my hand as I braved the pain. Daniel eyed the doctor to make sure his work was done to his standards. All three of us wondered if I would keep my foot. Eventually, I passed out from the pain, only to wake up in my own bed, with my foot still intact and fresh bandages wrapped around my ankle, thanking God for a loving brother and sister.

At least that's what my stupid six-year-old brain thought it saw. In reality it happened much, *much* differently.

It's true, I did get my foot stuck in the spokes of my brother's bike, but I never went to the hospital. My sister did freak out, but for a different reason. My brother gently took the bike off my legs and unwrapped my foot from the spokes, while reminding me that I was supposed to keep my feet *away* from the tires. An ambulance was never called. Daniel and my sister carried my body into the random house of a stranger who had seen the accident. The hospital bed was a stranger's kitchen table and the tweezers and scissors were from a manicure set. I don't remember waking up in my bed, but I do remember taking a bath that night and singing Frosty the Snowman to cope with the pain of my wound. Daniel and my sister were nervous, but not for my life. They were concerned for theirs.

The truth is, we were never going to see a movie. We were going to our cousin's house, which was behind Westlake.

Besides Daniel, we weren't even supposed to leave the house. So, the fact that we had left and that I had gotten hurt meant some serious trouble for my siblings. Like "go find your switch" and "I'm going to take off my belt" trouble. Little did they know, they actually shielded me from any wrongdoing by saying we were going to see a movie. I could claim ignorance. Of course, this wasn't revealed until I was older, so I have no idea what's truth and what's fiction; but it still makes me smile. It's a good story and a strangely happy memory. It's a memory before the fight between my brother and Dad resulted in Daniel moving out to live with my Aunt Jackie and Uncle Bobby during his senior year of high school. Before I was raped. Before my parents' divorce, the foreclosed house, and the eviction. Before living homeless for two years and the sinking depression that resulted in dropping out of college. Before the thoughts of suicide.

Then, it was just summer.

All I needed was my brother, sister, a bike, and a smile.

Men Can't Be Raped

I wish I had a better memory of what occurred the first time I was raped, but it's been over twenty years and some of the memories have become hazy. I do know the house was empty of my parents and brother. What's interesting is that the first time wasn't the first time. It began with my abuser and a pornographic tape. My abuser was my sister and, at the time, babysitter. I would often have a babysitter when Mom had to work late at Kmart, or Dad went out and had to DJ at the American Legion. My parents also simply went out sometimes (as parents should), or they didn't get home from work until after 5 p.m. So, during that time, when my sister and I were alone, is when the grooming began.

Grooming is not what you may think. It's not when two individuals sit down and brush and comb each other's hair like chimps in a zoo. Grooming is a term used to explain how abusers prepare their victims for molestation. For some abusers, it occurs when the victim runs around, becoming excited while playing tag, for example. Then, instead of continuing the game, the abuser grabs the genitals or breasts of his/her victim—anything to get the child sexually aroused and excited while making that victim believe he/she is safe and participating in a fun game. Afterward, the roles are reversed. The abuser has the victim run, tag, and touch him/her in the same way. This makes the victim believe this is how the game is played and allows the abuser to open the door to more egregious acts and games in which the abuser can easily sexually assault with less resistance and more severity.

My grooming occurred in the form of pornographic movies.

My dad had a collection of pornographic videocassettes under the mattress of the bed in our basement that were easily accessible and could easily be returned as if they had never been touched. Eventually, after the basement had been remodeled and the bed and mattress were thrown in the trash, the cassettes were moved to the bottom drawer of the desk in the basement.

The reason I remember this bed so vividly is because me, my sister, and Daniel would often play on the mattress when my parents were gone. Both would have me lie on the mattress while they ran and jumped on the bed to try and fling me into the air and against the wall. I loved it. It was just crazy, stupid, innocent stuff kids do when their parents are gone, unlike what eventually happened when Daniel moved away after physical fighting with my father.

The grooming began one afternoon when my parents were gone. I was being babysat, and she asked with a calm happy smile, after entering my room, "Hey, Kenny, wanna see something cool?" Of course, I agreed. I was eight-years-old. I lived for cool. Cool was my life, and she knew it.

From my room, she led me down to the basement, lifted up the mattress, removed the black cassette tape, and placed it in the VCR. I remember that the cassette wasn't labeled as pornography; instead it had a normal white label on the spine of the cassette, as if it had once been a different movie that had been taped over. Because it looked so similar to many other movies in our library, I never suspected its contents.

As the video had been paused in the middle of the cassette, it didn't start at the beginning. Instead, it continued from the last moment my father hit stop, which was in the middle of two people moving, groaning, and humping in ways I had no idea were possible at such an age. Immediately, I was disgusted. At the time, I didn't know what it was, but I knew it was a movie I was not supposed to watch. My eight-year-old brain flashed back to scenes of Spike Lee's *School Daze* and how my parents told me to cover my eyes during the "dirty parts." Seeing what was happening on the screen, I figured this was most definitely a "dirty part" that I wasn't allowed to watch, so I covered my eyes and waited for the okay that the scene had ended and I could open my eyes to something safe. Instead, she took my hands from my eyes and said, "Watch. It's funny." I tried to cover my eyes during a few scenes that followed that were especially embarrassing, but I was coaxed into watching.

Soon, it was over. When it came to an end, she rewound the tape to where it begun, put the cassette under the mattress, and went back upstairs to continue the day. Nothing happened. She did not try to touch me, or tell me to touch her. Rather than grooming me to become sexually aroused through a game that allowed us to explore each other's bodies, she groomed me to like the idea of sex through the use of movies, which were a primary source of entertainment in our house. Any free moment the family had was spent watching a movie. We all had our classic repeats that we could (and did) watch over and over again. My mother loved *Toy Soldiers*, *The Five Heartbeats*, and *The Temptations* Daniel loved *The Last Dragon*, I loved *The Rocketeer* and *Hook*, and my dad simply loved movies in general. Going to Blockbuster on Friday evenings to search the shelves for a new release or an unwatched classic was our regular routine. Because movies were such a large part of my family's life, pornographic movies could be made to seem like a safe, fun, and common form of entertainment that my eight-year-old self would never question as being invalid and unacceptable. It was a way to groom me.

Of course, I knew not to tell anyone about watching the videos. I was never told not to tell, but I just knew. Technically, nothing had happened, but I had been prepared by years of breaking figurines, rules, and going places that, when my parents left, what happened while they were gone was not discussed unless we were caught. It ensured that no one got in trouble. Unfortunately, my abuser never got caught.

For months, this is how it went. My parents would leave, she would get the tape from under the mattress; we would watch it, put it back, and continue with our day, never saying a word to our parents. The only other person to tell who could have stopped the abuse from happening was Daniel, who was eighteen-years-old and far away. After high school and attending Alabama A&M in Huntsville, Alabama for a year, Daniel dropped out of college, joined the military, and moved to Germany to raise a family of his own.

Although the grooming lasted for a number of months, it eventually turned to something much more sinister. As time progressed and the grooming continued, my abuser and I no longer sat on the floor together watching the video in silence, disgust, or mock laughter. Instead, each of us had our own positions in the room, separate from the other. She lay on the bed with a comforter over her body while I sat on the couch and watched the scenes play out on the screen. After months of watching the cassette in secret on weekends or late at night when our parents were gone, I no longer covered my eyes and looked away in embarrassment. In fact, most times I had become sexually aroused. My therapist tells me that this is normal—a natural reaction of the body to the stimulation of the brain. But I find it hard not to view myself as a protagonist of the sex and abuse, no matter what she tells me. However, I did not masturbate, mostly because I had no idea what masturbation was or that it was even possible. I was too young to know. My abuser on the other hand, being five years my senior, was discovering masturbation beneath the comforter on the mattress ten feet away, watching women receive pleasure from men in the same way she was sexually stimulating herself.

After being groomed to willingly watch pornography, remaining silent and sexually aroused while my sister was sexually stimulated through masturbation, all the pieces had fallen into place for me to be raped with little resistance and that's precisely what occurred.

The first time that grooming became rape, my abuser called me to the bed where she lay with the blanket pulled over her body. I looked at the bed and walked over. She said calmly but with a little hesitation, "Let's try something different. Get on top of me." This is when she pulled back the blanket to reveal she was wearing no pants or panties. Immediately, I froze. I had no idea what to say or do. I thought to myself, *Is this okay? Can I say no?* I wanted to say no, but I didn't know how. How could I? She was someone I trusted. I thought I had to do what she said. She was my sister. I believed with all my heart, beyond the shadow of a doubt, that she wouldn't do anything to hurt me. It's taken nearly thirty years, therapy, and meditation for this belief to finally change.

In the moment, she noticed my hesitation and knew she couldn't give me an option. With more confidence—invitingly but with more force—she said, "Let's do what they do. Come on," as she worked off my pants.

When the rape happened and she placed me on top of her, I didn't move. I lay there, lifeless, uncomfortable, and cold. She was larger and there was no way for me to touch the mattress, so I lay hovering in the air on top and inside her body as the pornographic movie continued to play in the background. When I didn't move, she became frustrated and annoyed that I wasn't doing it right. Again, she took control over the situation, grabbed me by the waist and made me move up and down, in and out, as she watched the scenes play out on the screen on the other side of the room. It lasted only a few minutes, but the impact has yet to vanish. She finished, and I stopped moving. We both got dressed, she rewound the tape, and put it back under the mattress as always. But this time was different. Rather than go upstairs to continue her day, she stopped and told me as she had never done before: "Don't tell."

"It's bad," she said, "and we'll get in trouble."

I was too young to argue, or know what it meant, so I didn't tell. I remained silent, just as she wanted. For over twenty years, I remained quiet because I didn't want to get in trouble; I thought, it was my fault and I'd be punished. There was nothing I could do if I didn't want Mom, Dad, and Daniel to look at me with the shame and regret I felt. I had done something wrong that no one knew had occurred except her, so the best and only option was to keep quiet and keep her secret.

How did this make me feel? In the moment, I felt dirty. I curled up inside myself, waiting for it to stop, and I haven't stopped waiting. I didn't say much. There was no kissing or fondling, just sex. And that's how it went for almost two years. Our parents would leave, pornography would play, I would be raped, and I wouldn't tell. Over time, I began to anticipate when it was going to happen, even look forward to it. My therapist says this is natural. She says it's normal to have been aroused and sexually stimulated. It's something the body does and something I couldn't control, but it still doesn't change what I feel—that it was my fault. That I could have stopped it. That I enjoyed it. That I'm to blame and, that no matter what I do, I'm damned beyond the reach of forgiveness.

Then, one day, abruptly, the rapes stopped. After church, she told me we couldn't do it anymore because it was wrong and that it never happened. I said okay, but my mind was racing. One thought after another came into my mind without stopping. *You did this to me and now you're saying we can't do it anymore? And you're telling me it never happened? You're telling me it was wrong - how wrong was it? Why was it wrong? What's going to happen to me if someone finds out?* It wasn't until much later that I would find answers to any of these questions.

You may be wondering why the rapes abruptly came to an end. I have asked the same question. I believed for years that she had an epiphany, realizing that she was psychologically, physically, and morally damaging someone she was supposed to love and protect. But the truth is much more logical and hurtful. I had become too old and was no longer useful. In the two years since this all began, I had gone from an eight-year-old child to a ten-year-old prepubescent boy who could get my fifteen-year-old sister pregnant. Pregnancy meant being discovered and this was something she could not allow to happen. So, instead, she told me it was wrong and brought it to an end, leaving me broken and confused, with no help of understanding the incest that had occurred. She allowed the thought that would mature into a belief and eventually become a cold hard fact in my mind: men can't be raped.

Our culture and society implicitly communicates, through its celebration of hyper-masculinity and clichéd ideas of what it means to be a man, that rape is an impossible fate for a red-blooded, heterosexual male. There's no way you can be the victim of sexual assault, unless you are a woman or a homosexual. These beliefs, seen through the eyes of the warped and damaged ego of a perpetual eight-year-old, help to create the negative view of myself I have today. A view I attempt to conquer once a week at therapy, like Quixote's ever-shifting and fictional windmills.

It is the belief of our society that the raping of males never occurs because the sexual abuse of males is hardly ever reported, no matter what the age. Therefore, it seemingly does not exist. Male survivors of sexual assault, meanwhile, suffer under the assumption that they're the only male to have been raped, leaving them feeling helpless, alone, damaged, and refusing to seek help. It leaves survivors like myself feeling inadequate as men and human beings, with serious psychological consequences.

In no way am I asking for the spotlight to be taken from female rape survivors. However, when rape of females does tragically occur, women usually know they are not alone. They know they're not the first, and, unfortunately, will not be the last. This doesn't rebuild the ego they were stripped of after being violated, but it can make seeking help more conceivable. Getting help is key to becoming healthy, and that is why I hope other male survivors read my story. Male survivors need to know they're not alone. They need to stop blaming themselves for what was done to them. They need to know that they did nothing wrong.

Rape is about power, control, and dominance—nothing else. It has nothing to do with sex. The abuse of male survivors is no different and neither was mine. To fully understand how this abuse was about power and control, you have to understand the history of my abuser and how it all began.

My abuser—my sister—was, like me, raped by her babysitter, Mr. Miller, probably around the same age that I was raped by her. When sexual abuse occurs at such a young age, the ability to feel safe and in control is stripped from the victims, leaving their psychological development stagnant between the ages of seven and nine. At this age, healthy individuals learn to gain independence, explore the world on their own, and take control of their environment. However, when an individual is raped at this age, such independence and control is stunted, leaving the child frozen in that early stage of psychological development. It is possible to progress through the other stages of development, but that stage will remain underdeveloped until help is sought and the wound can be healed properly. This means that without therapy and help, the rape victim will always feel as though they have no control over their life or their surroundings. This is why rape is so powerful. It allows the abuser to seemingly take back some of the control that was taken from them, continuing the cycle and perpetuating more and more rape until help is sought and the cycle is broken. This is what happened to my abuser.

At thirteen she was overweight, bullied, and felt as though she had lost all power in every aspect of her life. Being unable to seek help because of her embarrassment or fear of repercussions, she attempted to take back some control in the form of food—eating what she wanted, when she wanted. It was one of the few things that gave her pleasure and contentment. Unfortunately, gluttony was a bandage too small to deal with her psychological wound. The resulting obesity made her directionless, exposing her to bullying and rejection.

Her emotions of helplessness and powerlessness led her to sexually abuse *me* for a number of reasons. The primary reason was that I was the youngest. As the baby of the family, I could easily be groomed and manipulated into doing what she wanted. This also meant that she gained power through my weakness. Her dominance continues to this day and is one of the primary reasons that we no longer speak. By raping me, she stripped me of my ego, leaving me perpetually eight-years-old, seeking approval without the strength or ability to say no or stand up for myself. Regaining my ego is what I struggle with in therapy. It wasn't until recently that I stopped sympathizing with my abuser and saw the years of rape for the vile acts they truly were.

Being the youngest of three also meant that I received the most attention. Generally, I was well-liked and accepted by my parents and brother. I was funny, happy, smart, and kind, while it seemed she was none of the above. Seeing these qualities in me and not in herself may have ripped her insides to shreds. I was everything she wanted to be, but physically and mentally couldn't be. So she pulled me down. By raping me, she ensured I would always stay in my place and that she would always have the upper hand. It gave her the control over me that she always wanted over her own life. Years after the rapes had come to an end, the mental abuse continued.

You may be wondering, was this planned? When she sat me down and put the VHS into the VCR, did she consciously intend to regain the control she had lost by taking mine? No, I don't believe so. Not then. However, now, I believe she does realize what she is doing. Throughout her adult life, she has sought to control, manipulate, and dominate every situation and relationship. Rather than seek help, she has continuously

25

worsened over the years; I fear for the mental health and stability of my nieces and nephew. Without help, her unstable personality will pass to her children through her words and behavior.

If rape and sexual abuse is all about power, dominance, and continuing the cycle, why haven't I become an abuser? Why am I not a sex offender? Honestly, there is no logical reason. According to my therapist, many people with my background are addicted to drugs; victims of alcohol abuse; struggling in education; and unable to sustain lasting, stable, and healthy relationships. Yet, I've never done a drug in my life (besides the 20 mg. of Lexapro for my depression and anxiety), I drink no more than two beers before falling asleep, I have both a bachelor's degree from Bowling Green State University and a master's degree from Johns Hopkins University, and I am a happy father and husband who could never dream of sleeping anywhere besides his own bed or the couch in my daughters' room if one of them were sick. There is no logical reason that I have patience or pleasure in working with some of the most annoying, frustrating, and coolest people on the planet – seventh graders. The only explanation is that I am truly blessed. My therapist believes that I have somehow been able to compartmentalize the abuse. She's not sure how, but I have a theory.

When I was younger, and even to this day, I loved superheroes. Then, and now, I adhered to what they stand for. In the realm of comic books, there was no gray; there was only black and white, right and wrong. I wanted to be on the side of light and good, and the only way I knew to do that was by trying to be perfect in every way. I could strive to be kind, intelligent, sympathetic, moral, and adhere to a code of honor.

These beliefs about how to live and treat the people around me have stuck with me to this day. It's why I wrote my senior thesis on the evolution of chivalry through the ages—its representation and embodiment in knights, and the eventual replacement of knights by superheroes. This is the reason it took a year of therapy once a week before I stopped sympathizing with my abuser. In my mind, hating her was wrong because hate is wrong and she was a relative. I believed she needed understanding until she found her way. However, my attitude to her has now changed. I know everyone is responsible for their own actions. And it is the thought of my nieces and nephew, writing these same words and going through these same struggles from a person who never received help because I remained silent, that pushed me to put my own story to paper.

I run, meditate, read, and go to church to not be the person/thing that I fear I will become. The cycle of abuse won't continue with me. But my abuser has made sure that I never get to know the eight-year-old boy that I have locked away in a room deep in the recesses of my mind.

Action Guy (Fiction)

This is my room. I got toys! I got lots of toys! Not as many as before, but I still got toys. And they're not as new as they used to be. This one's broken, but that's okay. I still like it without the siren. I don't need a siren as long as it still rolls. I can make the siren noise. See. *Wrrrr!* Got to put out the fire! Hurry! *Wrrrr!* See, it still works, even without the siren. I got other toys though. I got a sail boat, a wagon and ... oh, Action Guy! I love Action Guy! He can do everything: Fly, SWWIISSHH; beat up bad guys, BANG POW; burst through walls, BOOM; and go wherever he wants by just thinking it. I wish I had that power. If only I could just close my eyes really tight, think really hard about some place far, far away, and POOF, be there. Anywhere! On a mountain, in the sky, in China, anywhere! That would be so cool. To go outside. I used to go places like Action Guy; I used to run in the grass and stuff, play, but not anymore. Not with the door locked. The door is always locked, at least now. It wasn't before. Before the bad thing, before ... before the walls used to be blue, bright blue.

And I had lots of toys. New toys with sounds, and lights, and cool bright colors. There was carpet, and outside my windows I could see clouds and sky and grass and sun. It was fun! But now ... now it's different since the bad thing. I'm not supposed to talk about the bad thing. It's not like it used to be since it happened. The walls are dirty and faded. The carpet is gone and the wood is hard and cold and creaks when I walk. And the clouds are gone. The windows are bricked up and I only have one tiny little hole to look through. And I can't see anything through it. Only sun. One small dot of sun. My toys are old and no one comes to see me. I'm always the only person here. I like to play by myself, but sometimes . . . sometimes I wish I had someone else to make the siren noise, and I didn't always have to make believe to be happy.

No one ever let me out after the bad thing. After she made me do stuff I didn't wanna do. I didn't want to play that game anyway. She made me! She said it would be fun! It wasn't fun! It was never fun. It was scary and made me feel bad. She made me touch . . . and . . . and to get on top of her. I didn't want to. I never wanted to. But I did. So I got in trouble. I got locked in here for being bad. It's my fault. I shouldn't have done it. Now I'm being punished. No more toys, no more clouds, or sun, or fun stuff. It's all my fault. Now I'm being punished. No more toys, no more clouds, or sun, or fun stuff. It's all my fault. Now I have to wait for someone to unlock the door. They'll come. I know they will. Action Guy will come and break down the door, kick out the bricks in the windows, and grab my hand. And then we'll squeeze our eyes together really tight, like this, and then POOF, we'll be outside in the sun, flying all day. And it won't be my fault anymore and the bad thing will be over.

But . . . but the door is still locked and Action Guy hasn't come yet, so I guess . . . I guess, I'll wait and play by myself. Like I always do.

Fifty Shades of Insanity

What do Disney's *Frozen* and E.L. James's *Fifty Shades of Grey* have in common? Hear me out before you judge. No, it's not the beginning of some disgusting joke. It's mental illness.

For those of you who may have been living under a rock, on Mars, or in an alternate dimension of Michio Kaku, and know nothing of the phenomenon that is *Frozen*, let me outline the plot of this Disney masterpiece.

Picture this. In the ancient mythical land of lederhosen, tubas, and wooden shoes, stood a kingdom. In this kingdom lived two beautiful princesses, Elsa, the oldest, and Anna, the lovable baby sister. Anna was normal, with no magical powers; she had braided red hair, humorous innocence, freckles, and white (but still tanned) skin. Anna loved life, all those around her, and idolized her older sister, Elsa. On the other hand, Elsa was very different; and it was not just her pale but beautifully flawless skin and gorgeous blond hair. Elsa had the ability to manipulate the weather and the surrounding atmosphere to create objects made of snow and ice with the flick of her wrist. These objects include a living snowman named Olaf and a giant snow monster named Marshmallow. I don't know how she is able to give life to inanimate objects, but it's Disney, so just go with it.

The entire movie is enlivened with songs, love, betrayal, a reindeer, and the angry white cousins of the wolves from *Beauty and the Beast*. However, although the movie is about how true love conquers fear, it's also about mental illness. At least, it is to me.

After seeing the movie more times than I can remember with Mirus, my oldest daughter, I've come to interpret Elsa's fear of her powers hurting the people around her a little differently than the average toddler. In the movie, after Anna sings a heartfelt song about how Elsa doesn't have to be alone, Elsa hits Anna with a snow blast to the heart, turning her into a statue of flawless ice for all of time, unless the spell is reversed by an act of true love.

After a very stressful afternoon with her sister, Elsa paces throughout her newly formed palace of clear-blue ice, worried, stressed, filled with anxiety, and frightened of the power she can't hide or control. As she pulls her hair and mumbles to herself, the once beautiful clear ice of the palace turns black, red, and purple as fractures appear deep beneath the surface, only to immediately refreeze, permanently sealing the fractures in place. As this happens, she continues to mumble, over and over again, "Conceal, don't feel. Conceal, don't feel!" But it doesn't work. In fact, it only gets worse. The more she tries to fight the fear of everyone knowing who she truly is and of letting people down, the stronger it grows. This, ladies and gentlemen, is depression.

Like Elsa, everything I did (running, writing) and everything I tried (mentally beating myself with the accusation that my best wasn't good enough) was to keep my fear and anxiety locked down deep inside. I told myself over and over again, *Hide it. Don't let people see. If they see it, they won't accept you. They won't understand. Keep the secret.* While I concealed the fear, more fractures appeared and froze beneath the surface of my consciousness, leaving scars locked in place until the thaw of spring. The only problem was that spring never came. I searched desperately for an answer on my own, moving from one place to another, trying to keep busy while becoming more lost and afraid every minute. I didn't get help. Eventually, with enough fractures, I broke.

The thoughts of being raped at eight-years-old (fracture), living homeless for two years (fracture), and dropping out of college and feeling worthless (fracture) had all been pushed down deeply in my mind. I tried to forget and move on, keeping the secret for over twenty years in order to protect the people I cared about. Through elementary, middle, and high school; college; and into adulthood, I kept telling myself, *Shut up! There's nothing wrong! Get over it!* But I could not feel. Humans are meant to feel. Emotions are programmed into our DNA. Hiding and concealing only creates a dam that eventually has to burst. And that's precisely what happened. It took a decade, but the levies finally broke when I was twenty-nine-years-old, leaving me mentally crippled and unable to function.

Months before my breakdown, I had gone through the process of buying my first home, finished graduate classes at Johns Hopkins University, left one dysfunctional school in Baltimore to work at a highly functional charter in the city, and had my firstborn daughter, Mirus. It seemed that the world was my oyster, moments before it came crashing down in anxiety, fear, and depression. I continued journaling through the breakdown, hoping it would keep me sane and prevent me doing something stupid. For the most part, it worked. The following chapter is the result of that writing.

The Journal

What to write?

There's too much reality. Too many things I *have* to do.

The problem is there's no magic in the world. No spectacular, no awesome. There's only the simple. The ordinary. The everyday. When I see colors they're orange, green, and blue. I see the sunlight and I know it's supposed to be there. I know the warmth, but it's not enough. There should be more. *There* NEEDS to be more.

There's something wrong with me. Really wrong!

It feels like I have nothing to look forward to. This morning in the shower, standing there, letting the water run over my body, I tried to think of something that brought or would bring me joy. There was nothing. Seeing Mirus this morning smile and playing just brought tears to my eyes.

All I do now is cry, lay in bed and let the tears fall because I can't find a reason to get up.

Standing.

Sitting.

Moving.

They all seem too difficult in the dark, but light seems too far away. Almost as if it would hurt. I like the dark, but I know it's paralyzing. Keeping me trapped in my own thoughts behind closed eyes. I don't want to open them. All there is is what I already have. Everything I've seen.

Nothing new.

No new experiences.

No new happiness.

Just the same day in and day out.

***

Cardboard

Opening eyes and seeing the steps, he was careful not to fall through the stiff, black cardboard.

He touched the white paper walls and brown paper banister. In the darkness he turned on the light. Flicking the switch like the snap of a rubber band.

The first landing was more sturdy, so he walked with ease toward the white papered door and stiff cardstock handle. Gently, so not to break through like he had countless times before, he turned the handle and entered the blue and green construction paper room. Brown paper wrapped the small couch to the left, and sitting there, smiling with the sight of his face was his flesh and blood, living, breathing, and happy daughter that he loved with all his paper heart.

With hands and fingers of wrapping and newspaper he reached to pick her up. Fragile fingers touched her living body and gave way to the weight. Drooping, sagging to the floor as he lifted with all the might the paste of his shoulders would allow. Each arm almost fell from his body to the floor, and for a moment he thought they would, but they held.

She nestled into his chest, denting the paper and plastic padding. There was no pain. There was nothing. Only the crackling of his flesh under her weight. The baby sought comfort and found it. He sat, battered, bruised, and dented on the four legs of the couch. She curdled into a ball and slept in the mass of tissue paper and padding that was her father. Together they rested. Him pleased that he could at least give her a place to feel comfortable and happy, even if he had fallen apart in the process.

***

Just get through the day. That's all you have to do. Each and every day just stand up and walk through it. Arriving to meet it is half the battle.

It's true, I haven't stood up to meet the day these past few days, but I'll get back to where I was.

Don't think, just get up, get dressed, and get out the door. The rest will fall into place later.

There are places I wish I could go, but can't.

Just let go.

***

I got the medication today. Haven't taken it yet. Will it fix me? Probably not. Nothing can fix me. Only I can fix me. Going to the doctor today only sealed the deal that I just have to deal with this. No one can help.

Just remember there're only two cures. Just get through the day.

Daniel's talking about coming to visit. And Mom. Why do so many people keep making such a big deal about me? Just let me fall. Leave me alone. All I have is me. If I know that, if that stays plastered in the back of my mind with layers and layers of duct tape I'll be fine.

***

STOP!!!

Don't think about lessons tomorrow. Focus on . . . now. Anything other than that time in the future that hasn't come yet. It doesn't exist. What exists is this moment. Trust and believe in yourself and you can do anything.

***

Supernatural *is kind of depressing.*

Oct 8

A new day.

New medication.

I feel . . . better. I'm just afraid that this feeling will go away. The fear I had, the unknowing fear of what was soon to come just ate away at me. Now, I just feel better.

I took the day to make sure I feel better.

I'm watching *Mr. Nobody* and I'm afraid that I'm going to become like Elise, crazy and hurting the people around me.

But, I also don't feel bad about who I am and what I've done. I need to get better. There's nothing wrong with taking the time to take care of yourself.

Heal.

Regenerate.

That's what I'm doing. Regenerating. Becoming something better. Now, I can still try and accomplish as much, but without all the effort.

It's okay. Everything is going to be okay. However, don't forget the feeling. Keep it locked away, but keep the key. Never lose the key. Keep it to write about. Help others through the night to see the dawn.

Shit.

I think it's coming back.

My thoughts are beginning to circle again. No. No. No. I'm doing the right thing by taking the day. I emailed Katie. I let her know what I was doing. It's okay. Take care of yourself. Take care of yourself. Take care of yourself.

Be *sane* for Sarah!!

***

Suffered a low around 7:15. It's 7:40 and I haven't really recovered.

Anxious about what others will say. I tried to calm myself by thinking, *No, I'm doing this to get better*. Then I thought, *No, I'm already better. You feel better. You should have gone to work*. Maybe I should have gone to work. Everyone else made it to work. Why couldn't you? Everyone is judging you right now.

No. No. No!!

STOP!!

If I can't stop, then I'm going to take a pill.

It's just a fear that everything is falling apart.

Sleep!!

***

Sunlight filters through the open windows. Breeze after gentle breeze push and seemingly pull the sliding curtains into the room and against the wall, knocking their metal rims and filling the room with clanks and knocks with each intake and exhale of air. Outside, through the small window on the other side of the shower, leaves rustle and move. Shadows of black rest and move on top of branches of brown, leaves of green, and all encapsulated in gold behind a backdrop of emerald blue. Instead of the gentle song of loving birds it's the lull of passengers and drivers making their way past stop lights and street signs to be with family. All of them with their own destinations. All of them fighting, clawing, yearning to live as best they can.

It's all they can do.

It's all they wish to do.

Some succeed while others fail.

And some, a few, strive and stride towards more.

***

I'm not living up to expectations. I feel better now that I need to do it. The anxiety has flipped on its head. I can handle the classroom so that's where I should be. Now that I'm focusing on getting myself better it's stressing me out. I don't want to think about myself. In fact, I can't really think about myself right now. What I want doesn't matter. It doesn't matter. I don't matter. Sitting at home, waiting to heal is tying my stomach in knots, but I can't think of doing schoolwork. It's not supposed to be done here. For some reason I'm hooked up on rules again.

I need to move.

Get better.

There are things I need to do, have to do, that will make me better.

It's almost like I have to make it up to everyone. I HAVE to make it up for the way I've been behaving. I just don't want to sit around. I want to move and do what I have to. Become the person I was.

Sleep.

Exercise.

School.

Marriage.

Family.

I know what I have to do and I need to do it. Start doing what you need to do *now*! Don't wait!

***

Guilt. That's the emotion I have right now. Guilt for putting everyone in this situation. So much guilt for being selfish. I just want to go back, take on my responsibilities, and move back into the fray. Disappear as a worker with no issues.

It's just *stupid!!*

It's like I failed. I failed them all. There's no way to get back these days. I've failed everyone!!

I hate that bed! It traps me. It wraps its arms around me and suffocates until I can't breathe. It yells, calms, soothes, does anything and everything to get me under its covers where it paralyzes me.

I HATE IT!!

It wants me to not move. To stay there. *I* WON'T.

I let everyone down. I have to make it up. *I have* to!! It's not the end of the world. Time keeps moving. And I have to keep moving.

I'm better when I move. Much better!!

Becoming a Father

Looking back, I can see the parallels between myself and Elsa in *Frozen*. It's hard to read and know—that used to be me. That it's still me.

I know when my ice began to fracture, fall apart, and turn black. It all started the day I became a father.

To me, being a parent means having new and important responsibilities the moment your child comes into the world. Being a parent means (or is supposed to mean) protecting, loving, and providing no matter what the cost. It means trying desperately to shield your children from harm while preparing them for the hardships to come. So, when I held Mirus, my oldest daughter, for the first time and knew that this small person was my responsibility for the rest of my life, my subconscious went into overdrive, knocked on the wall of my conscious saying, *Can we have a talk? I'm running out of room over here and I would really love to clear some of this mess out.*

Nine months after Mirus was born, my world fell apart. I became anxious, scared, unsure, and terrified that I was making or going to make a mistake that would end my life and leave me and my family broken and homeless as I had been. I never felt safe. I woke up paralyzed by fear, crying and holding Sarah, trying every tactic I could to fool my brain into pulling itself from bed. Eventually, I couldn't. I went crazy. Getting out of bed became impossible. The fear of what the day held, and its unpredictability, made my heart feel as though it would jump out of my chest. So, I called off work. I took a mental health day. Then, I took another, and another, until, eventually, I felt completely worthless. There seemed to be only one logical answer to my problems. Suicide.

In my head, I was worthless. I couldn't do my job as a father, husband, or teacher so, I thought, I needed to die. And I should be the one to take my own life. It makes no sense now, but, then, it all clicked. There were no thoughts of the family I would leave behind, or the fact that suicide is a sin in the eyes of the church. All that mattered was ending my shame for what I thought were my shortcomings as a man, husband, and father, but were actually the result of being raped.

I was going to hang myself. I wanted it to hurt. I thought I deserved the pain. I wanted it to be slow, painful, and leave bruises so others could see me as worthless as I saw myself. I was going to do it in the bedroom closet. There was a metal bar that could support my weight, and it seemed peaceful. It never crossed my mind that Sarah would be the one to find me hanging there lifeless, and have no idea what to do, why I had done it, and whether or not there was anything she could have done to stop it from happening. Suicide hurts those left behind, leaving them with questions that can never be answered. But I didn't care. If there had been rope in the house, this story would never have been told. Instead of heading over to Ace and asking, "Hey, what's the thickest, most course, and cheapest rope you have in stock? Oh, and do any of you happen to know how to tie a noose?" I called a doctor.

Immediately, they connected me to a nurse. She wanted to send an ambulance, but I refused. It's weird, but I thought it was too much of a bother. If I was going to die, I didn't want to cause anyone any trouble. I said I could drive myself to the hospital myself, but someone had to take me because . . . you know . . . I wanted to kill myself. Instead, I called, Sully, a friend who's a firefighter. I told him what was happening and, without a moment of hesitation, he came and picked me up and took me to the emergency room. It was there that I told them I had been molested as a child. That's when the treatment began.

As I have said, after therapy, meditation, and medication, I have a better idea of what sent me flying off the deep end. After Mirus was born, I began asking questions that had no good answer. *Why didn't my parents keep me safe and protect me from being raped? What if Mirus is raped? How can I protect her when I couldn't even protect myself? Why did my abuser do this to me?*

However, the big question that I couldn't get out of my head, and still pops up every now and again when I change the diaper of my daughters, or give them a bath, or tickle them and give them a kiss on the cheek, is: *Will I sexually abuse my daughters?* I have an overwhelming fear that one day I'm suddenly going to transform from Dr. Jekyll into Mr. Hyde and hurt the people I have unconditional love for: Mirus and my youngest, Amare.

I couldn't let the question go. I still can't let it go. This thought sometimes keeps me from hugging them and makes me really, *really* freaked out when Mirus points at my crotch and says, "Pee. Pee." This is the worst repercussion of being sexually abused. She took away my ability to feel comfortable and safe loving my daughters. It's one thing that I don't think I will ever be able to forgive.

Now, *Fifty Shades of Grey.*

First, let me admit for the record that I have never read the book. Not even a page has passed before my eyes. All I know of the book is what I have seen of the cover, what NPR has told me, and what Sarah has explained to me about the plot. But I do know more about Mr. Grey from Sam Taylor Johnson's cinematic adaptation, and what I have seen is a man suffering from a horrible mental illness after being sexually assaulted as a child.

Again, if you have lived under a Martian rock in an alternate dimension, the plot of *Fifty Shades of Grey* is as follows: A female virgin named Anastasia Steele graduates from college, falls in love with a billionaire corporate Adonis named Christian Grey, who loves her, but wants to make her his submissive (sex slave). He beats, whips, gags, ties, plugs, and sexually dominates her in his "play room." (Surprisingly, this is a much easier plot to summarize than *Frozen*.)

While most women, couples, and men went to see the movie (or rent it on Netflix like I did) for the no-holds-barred, adrenaline thrilled, blind-folded, hands tied with his necktie, feet-cuffed sex scenes, there was something more to the movie that most critics overlooked. Christian Grey was sexually abused as a child and, because of this sexual abuse, he sought these sexually dominant forms of sex, which he even demanded of his romantic partners.

There's one scene in which Christian says to Anastasia, "I'm all kinds of fucked up," after she pressures him to have a normal relationship. Christian believes he can't have a normal relationship. He knows he's damaged goods. He believes with all his heart that there is no way anyone could love him if they knew not only everything that happened to him, but also everything he had been forced to do. It seemed so impossible to him that he refuses to even admit that he has sex. "I don't have sex, I fuck," he says early in the movie, even though he clearly makes love to Anastasia numerous times. The problem is that he sees himself as being unworthy of anyone's love. Just as I can relate to Elsa's depression, I can relate to Dorian's self-loathing. I see myself in the same way.

I love my wife and our two children, but, until recently, I didn't think I was deserving of their love. I don't even believe I'm deserving of God's love. When my family and I attend mass and the entire family goes up for either blessing or communion, I stay seated and pray. It's not because I'm not Catholic, but because I truly believe I'm eternally damned. Why? Because incest is a major sin and in my impaired brain, all of the rape and molestation was my fault because I was the male in the situation and, again, men can't be raped. Society has made me (and pretty much everyone else) believe that no matter the situation, when rape is involved, it's the male's fault. It's a thought I still struggle with in therapy. I tell my therapist that I understand it wasn't my fault, and I do, but in my mind, and it will always be there, *all of this was my fault.*

If I had just said no. If, after the abuse had been going on for months, I didn't begin to anticipate when the abuse was going to happen. If I had simply told my parents, then none of it would have happened and I wouldn't be "all kinds of fucked up," as Mr. Grey would put it.

But the reality, as my therapist is trying to make me understand, is that I am the only one in this entire situation who *wasn't* at fault. It's true, my abuser was raped when she was a child by her babysitter, Mr. Miller, but she continued the cycle. It's true, my mom didn't know it was happening every time she left us alone together, but she put me in that situation to be molested, over and over again. And my father was at fault for having pornography in the house that could be easily found and watched by his children, not to mention for creating a broken house. Both my parents were at fault for being so wrapped up in their marital problems that they ignored the serious problems of their children. It upsets me to write this, but it's true. I would love, in a heartbeat, to be able to take the blame for everything. I would if I could, but I can't. Sometimes, bad things happen and there's nothing we can do about it. We have no control. It's hard to admit, but the truth is usually the hardest to handle for everyone.

So, with that being said, who's the villain in this tale? Who's the Big Bad Wolf? Are these three people, who I love and care about, horrible people because of this one tragic incident that has altered my life? I don't think so, but that's the problem. This is life. There are no villains. Each of us is sinner and saint. We're human. All of them, all of us, including myself, tried the best we could with what we had at the time. My sister handled her rape by internalizing the pain, trying to push it out through food. She attempted to control every situation in order to fabricate the safety and control that had been taken away from her. I did the same when I strove toward perfect grades and perfect obedience of the rules in an attempt to control feeling safe. The only difference is that she continued the cycle when she refused to get help, while I went to therapy when I couldn't take handling the pain on my own. You determine the hero and the villain. Just remember, let he who has not sinned cast the first stone.

I don't hate any of them. But I have to write to tell a story that's haunted me for my entire life. This is not for them. This is not to ruin lives, seek revenge, or make them regret what has happened. This is for me. And my hope is that it helps someone else know that he doesn't have to be ashamed, keep his secret, and feel like he is less than human, as I did. My prayer is that this makes its way into the hands of someone who finds the courage to tell his own story and not be afraid of how the world may view him.

We all have our demons, but it's how we fight them that ultimately separates the saints from the sinners. Unfortunately, demons come in many forms—too many to count. They appear as people, places, and emotions we once trusted. The only way I've found to fight and sometimes win is through fiction and words, revealing who these demons truly are, and unmasking the fear, before finding my way back home. This is why I include my fiction. This is why I write. It's my attempt to take back the control that was taken from me.

Needs (Fiction)

Slowly, black numbers on a white background rolled one after the other before slowing to a stop, and the mid-sized sedan pulled up to a pump at an illuminated gas station. Orbs of light hovered above, shining on a single pump marked with the label *unleaded gasoline.*

Snow layered atop a flat roof, sheltering the ground below.

Within seconds, the car was parked and the ignition silenced. The door opened, wind blew from the darkness, unsettling snow and blistering skin.

Door closed.

Compacted snow crunched beneath hard-soled shoes.

Gas flowed.

The tank filled.

White indentations led from car bumper to sliding doors.

A single digital chime filled the air as doors slid on grooves, parting on either side, exposing unrestrained light, radiating heat, and warmth enclosing five aisles of multi-colored, freeze-dried goods; five refrigerated coolers of soft drinks, milk, beer, and processed cheese; and racks of magazines, menthol packages, and scented cigarettes.

Doors slid shut, enclosing heat.

Outside, snow continued to fall, thick and heavy. Eyes moved from one side to the other, inspecting plastic packages and synthetic flavors, before settling on the outline of a man encased in a green shirt, white buttons, khaki pants, and brown belt.

The man stood behind the counter, motionless, and arms down, with a face filled with a superficial smile and the monotonous white teeth of a used-car salesmen.

"Hello, Sir. What is it I can help you find?"

The traveler, still slightly chilled from the outside air, stepped from the black mat beneath his feet, across the checkered tile floor, to the smooth surface of the countertop where he rested his hands. One looked into the eyes of the other with an expression of inquisition, the other stood with lifeless eyes and a charmless grin.

"Hi. I was wondering . . ."

"Hi," the employee said, cutting the voice of the traveler in half, preventing him from continuing. The smile remained on his face.

"Hi . . . umm, I've been on the road for . . ." The man paused as if he had forgotten his train of thought, or even his name. The employee said nothing, only continued to smile. The traveler attempted to finish his sentence but was unable.

"I've been on the road for . . . How long have I been on the road?" He paused for a moment, searching his memory without result. He stared at the fingers of his hands in contrast to the green countertop they rested on, hoping they would provide the answers he searched his mind to find.

"I stopped for gas in . . ." No memories surfaced. "That is so weird. I can't remember how long I've been driving. I can't even remember where I'm coming from. All I can remember is the storm . . . and the snow . . ."

The employee stood silent and still, wearing the same unaltered smile.

"I'm sorry," the traveler attempted to smile, but found himself unable. "As I was saying, I've been traveling for so long, and the storm . . . the storm seems to be never-ending, and . . . the point I'm trying to make is, I don't know where I am."

Both men waited for the other to speak, with the sound of motors cooling refrigerators, and snow blowing through the darkness. The traveler was unsure of where or how to continue.

"Can you help me?"

"With what?" The smile remained.

"With where I am."

"What are you trying to find?"

"Find?" The traveler paused, but for only a moment. "I don't know," he searched for answers without result. "I never thought about what I was trying to find."

He stood, staring into the hapless grin of the employee, before responding with one word.

"Home."

With the utterance of the word, lights flickered off throughout the room and across the garage, leaving all in the darkness of the night. And, for only an instant, he could feel the cold winter wind blow through his body, leaving a hollow sensation of loneliness, as lights and warmth returned to the room.

On the face of the employee, the smile had transformed into a grimace. It was present for only a moment, but in that moment of full brightness something had changed. Both the traveler and the employee knew their needs, and it became their wants.

"I'm trying to get home."

The smile broadened.

"I understand, Sir. But what is it that you are trying to find?"

"I'm not sure I understand. What I'm trying to find? I'm not trying to find anything. At least, I don't believe I am."

Both men stood in front of the other, inches apart, separated by polished brass and painted plywood.

"Of course you are. Everyone who arrives is searching for something. Even if they don't know it, they are. And it is part of my job, my responsibility, to help them find it."

"But, I don't think I'm trying to find anything. Just a way to get home."

The employee's smile faded. "No." The word was hard, forceful, and unforgiving before the smile returned. "Just ask yourself what you need."

The man stood, staring into the perfectly polished floor before raising his gaze to the employee's white smile once more.

"I don't need anything. I just want to get home."

"I know you do," said the employee, moving from behind the counter to the traveler's side. "But you can't get there."

"Excuse me?"

"Without food. You can't get anywhere without food in your system. When was the last time you ate?"

The employee stood beside the man with the same eerie smile that did not ease the tension of the moment. Snow continued to layer the ground as its flakes fell from the night sky.

"I can't remember."

"Exactly. Follow me."

Turning from the man dressed in winter clothing, with melted snow dripping from his jacket to the floor, the employee dressed in landscape green led him down the center aisle, revealing rows of packaged goods on either side. They came to a stop in the center of labels and marketable goods of mass consumption. They stood beside each other, staring at all that surrounded them.

"Choose." One word was all the nameless employee said before walking away.

The traveler turned towards the end of the aisle where the employee stood with the same smile that never seemed to leave his face. "We will discuss payment when you return to the counter." And with those words he was out of sight.

The traveler returned his eyes to the aisle of products stretching out under the number three, which dangled from above on partially invisible fishing wire.

Plastics lined makeshift shelves.

Compressed corn-filled, vacuum-sealed bags.

Unpronounceable text-lined, colored bags.

Bars of chocolate, containers of candy, tubes of sweets, and jerked meat were arranged by color, size, brand, and price. All were different, but the same in their foreign appearance and seemingly alien texture. None seemed appetizing, but still the man knew he needed to choose if he wanted to ever return home.

He reached for a package, but as he did, it was snatched from him.

He reached for another and, again, it was taken.

A sea of bodies was now moving with a hurried pace through the aisles, creating a blurry haze of gray carts on black wheels and oiled axels. Voices filled the air. Murmuring mothers and fathers, sighing sons and daughters, longing lovers, and close friends pondered prices and debated colors as the man continued down the never-ending aisle. None of the strangers looked at each other for more than a moment, if at all. But they all moved, taking product after product from the shelves, replacing some and emptying others.

To his right, kneeling beside price points, facing understocked items, and hoisting displays, of consistently shifting commercialized capitalism were men and women in orange vests, carrying black guns loaded with orange stickers. Most stood silently, staring at metallic cans, green vegetables, cotton lining, wooden surfaces—moving each to new places and moving them back, before taking them all away and replacing them completely. Some spoke with each other, whispering instructions and indicating directions that needed following.

Once assembled, thoroughly cleaned, and vacated of sales associates, customers swarmed, taking seemingly new products of fresh paint and glossy exteriors while leaving outdated merchandise of last month's design and color to leave gaping hollow hopes that needed filling.

As the traveler walked, he no longer reached for merchandise on bright attractive shelves. He looked into the customers' faces, attempting to make eye contact. None looked in his direction. None spoke when he asked directions or asked where he was; he continued to walk.

Soon, directly in front of his aisle, spelled out in bright, red letters was the word: EXIT.

His pace quickened.

The traveler ran towards the sign, passing mindless individuals paying him no attention. Reaching the end of the aisle did not bring checkout lanes or more endless aisles extending in either direction into oblivion. All it brought was darkness, a single cream painted door, and a silver hooked handle. Pulling the handle, the traveler stepped through the door and entered the smooth exterior of a painted wall and grey tile. The shuffling sound of the movement of bodies, wheels, and price guns came to a stop as the door swung on its hinges, latching shut with a final click of the lock.

Past five aisles of products, five large coolers, and a single counter the traveler approached the electronic sliding doors of the convenience store towards the snow, the cold, and his car. Before glass could move, and heat and will could escape, the cashier appeared, revealing green shirt and contrasting white smile. The traveler stopped, but did not turn.

"Did you find what you needed?" Despite the smile, his tone had changed, revealing more condescension and hatred than before.

The traveler's eyes remained on the night, and the swirling flakes falling from the darkness above. He paused for a moment, staring, and attempting to understand something he could not fully grasp as thoughts mingled with confusion. Looking out, he suddenly felt an urge, a pull from something in the darkness; something unknown but as attractive and irresistible as gravity. With the world silent, and the sky falling to the ground, the traveler spoke.

"I . . . I think . . ." the traveler stumbled as if making up his mind. "I think I'm going to get back on the road."

"You can't leave," said the cashier with the same unaltered smile. "Not until you've found what you need."

"I don't *need* anything. Not here," the traveler said towards the glass and darkness. "What I need is out there, on the road. I need to find my way home."

Putting his hands on the shoulders of the traveler, the cashier turned the man from the door back towards the artificial light and warmth of the store. The traveler did not resist.

"Now, if I had to guess," said the cashier, "I would have to say you were pretty tense. This is no way to drive through the night. Am I right?"

The traveler said nothing. The cashier continued to smile. Just as before, they walked down aisle three.

"I don't need food," the traveler said immediately, stopping and beginning to turn back towards the door.

"Of course you don't," said the cashier while keeping his grip on the man's shoulder, forcing him to step further from the doors and into the store. "What you need is something much more essential, basic. You need sustenance, hydration. Something to whet your whistle, put you at ease, and send you on your way. Right?"

The traveler paused, thinking, searching for answers which now seem to elude his mind. The pull he felt moments ago now seemed distant and imaginary, causing him to question his own beliefs.

"I ... don't ..."

"Of course you do." Before the traveler could finish, the cashier made up his mind for him. He knew he had already won.

They stood before five large coolers lining the back wall.

"Now choose." The smile of the cashier faded, causing lights to flicker and ice to fill the room before warmth, lights, and the smile returned as quickly as they had left. The cashier's hand left the traveler's shoulder. When he turned, the cashier was gone.

He turned back to the gleaming glass and un-smudged handle of the door. The overhead lights illuminated row upon row of plastic bottles behind the doors: citrus liquids infused with lime; brown cola carbonated, with red caps; juices of purple, red, and clear brown. He looked at them all, studying each price marked with black labels. Some indicating sales for a multiple purchase he did not want.

This was not what he wanted. He simply wanted to return to his car and continue on his journey home. Exhausted with choices, the man pulled on the silver handle, unleashing the sound of fans and the sensation of chilled water vapor. Cold, he pulled out a clear, unmarked bottle of water, stepped back, and let the stainless steel door of the refrigerator echo through the room.

Holding the clear liquid in his hand, the traveler looked from one side of the room to the other. Cupboards of colorless white extended to the ceiling from the raised tile floor. But the center of the room now contained a smooth board of grey granite, and pots and pans descended from the ceiling.

Lighting was dark. The room was hot, too hot for the coat and extra layers on his body. But still he kept them on, unsure of his surroundings. Like the bottle in his hand, his head began to sweat.

"Hello?"

His voice echoed throughout the empty home, ricocheting off immaculate walls down the single hallway shrouded in darkness.

"Is anybody here?"

Again he spoke with only his question as a reply. Speckles of water dripped from his hand to the floor.

"I'm looking for a way home."

No movement.

No life.

Only himself and the deserted home.

Placing the bottle on the counter top, the man stepped across scuffed, tiny tiles to the single hall in hopes of finding an exit.

Stepping into the hall, the traveler did not find the immediate darkness he expected. Instead, a white glow filled the hallway, illuminating the walls.

He continued forward.

Past bare walls which appeared grey in the dim light, he walked. He looked at the ground and saw that wooden floorboards had replaced the tile floor of the kitchen. He looked back, for only a moment, and saw nothing in his past except an abyss of darkness. He did not speak, fearing his voice would be taken and never returned.

He continued forward.

The light grew stronger.

On each side of the hallway there were no doors, no windows, and no mirrors—only the grey glow of lifeless walls, and the silence of his muffled footsteps on the hardened ground. As he continued to move forward, the glow filled the hallway and revealed the entry of a door-less frame.

He stepped forward.

Carpet formed around the sides of his shoes as he took three steps and stopped. Before him was a single bed. Its sheets were spread and tucked along the sides of the full-size mattress. Two pillows rested along the dark, wooden headboard that matched the surrounding frame. The four corners of the bed sunk into the floor, hiding its edges beneath the carpet's fluffy epidermis. In the corner was a television, boxed, large, with wooden panels of a different complexion from the bed. It was lighter, synthetic, fake. It was as if it did not belong.

Static filled the screen.

The volume was silenced.

Like the hallway, the walls were empty. And he knew that the hallway, like the kitchen, was now dark. There was no place to go. He stepped closer to the bed before he stopped and stared into the screen. His eyes locked on the glass and did not look away.

In the static, he knew; he remembered. He had found what he needed.

He stepped toward the television screen, staring at the white insects of static that roamed across it, listening as compacted snow crunched beneath his feet. He took another step, feeling the cold wind on his face, blowing through his bones as he walked towards his car.

Previous footprints were no longer present. Each was covered with drift and accumulation. He stepped past the front bumper to the car door as lights above flickered off one by one. He closed the door to darkness and silence. Before him was the light of the convenience store. Inside he could see merchandise lining the shelves. Through the glass, he could see the green shirt and khaki pants of the white-grinned employee standing at the counter, waiting for the next customer.

He turned the ignition; with a flick of his wrist the headlights of his car appeared, and the building before him vanished into darkness. Park went to drive, and the odometer slowly began to rotate.

BLACK

The worst thing that happens to you may be the best thing for you if you don't let it get the best of you. – Will Rogers

How Black Are You?

The idea of blackness never goes away. The question is always there. Am I black enough? And many times, the answer is no, I'm not, but I am me. Accepting the fact that I love going for a run when I've had a hard day, and that being on the Bowling Green State University Speech and Debate Team comes to mind rather than going to crazy parties, makes me happy. The truth is, I'm a nerd; there's nothing I can do about it, and there's nothing wrong with it. Although, going to therapy has recently made me question that.

You see, when a person is raped at such a young age and has no way of dealing with the pain, it creates a form of post-traumatic stress. When the act occurs, it takes control away from the individual, leaving them feeling helpless, whether they know it or not. It makes them feel as if nothing is under their control; they live in a state of fear. This fear leaves them with two options.

Option 1: Give in. The victim self-medicates in the form of alcohol, cigarettes, drugs, sex, or all of the above. His ability to make rational decisions has been taken along with his sense of control. He is lost and has no way of finding himself. Many of the decisions he makes about his life, job, and relationships seem wrong to others because they are. Decisions are foreign and he goes through life making one poor decision after another without truly knowing why, unless he seeks help.

Option 2: Control everything. The victim thinks, and so feels, that because control was taken away from him, he must attempt to control everything in his life, leaving nothing to chance. Such an individual is very responsible and deathly afraid of the unknown. He fears making the wrong choice and losing the little control he has, so he over-plans. He gives everything a specific spot that can't be moved. He tries to live his life as perfectly as possible, based on what he sees others doing because that is all he knows. This kind of victim is also lost in the dark, but he follows the flashlights of others to try and find an exit. Rather than alcohol, he shields himself with attempts to be intellectual and always in control of the situation.

My personality steered me towards the latter.

Knowing this made me question if any of my choices where my own. It made me wonder if the life I chose was really in my control. Do I really love to read or is that just an auto-defense mechanism to try and have some control over my life when control was taken away from me? Am I really responsible with money or am I just afraid of making wrong decisions with my money? Am I supposed to be a teacher, or am I meant to be in L.A. or New York making it as a professional actor? All of these questions have gone through my head. I even question whether or not I was supposed to be married to Sarah or whether it was my mind choosing to date white women all these years because it was a black girl that raped me. What was the truth? There is one thing I do know after dwelling and meditating on the issue: this is the life I've chosen. The friends I have, the family I have created, and the life I've built was done by me. And it's because of this life that I have changed and helped the lives of many young people I have taught, coached, and come in contact with. It's because of this life that I have a lovely daughter that makes me smile and brings peace to the people she meets. In the beginning, I may not have had a choice over my life. Something may have been taken away that altered the way I saw the world, but I could have chosen to drown my problems in cigarettes and alcohol rather than a long run and self-reflection. There was another option and I chose the more responsible one. That means something. So, whether I act too white, or I'm not black enough, means nothing when compared to the fact that I'm me, and that's all that truly matters. At least, that's all that matters to me now. Before, being black meant something much, much, *much* different.

Gay or Marry a White Woman

It all began in the nineties.

It was the R&B golden age of silk shirts, Captain Planet, and TGIF. They were ten years of adolescence spent walking the halls of Woodrow Wilson Elementary and Sterling Middle in Peoria, Illinois, in which I questioned (and hated) each and every thing about each and every thing, like every other pre-teen that came before and will come after.

No matter your age, gender, ethnicity, blood-type, or sperm count, you know it's true. From age seven to whenever we decide the world isn't out to get us, we hate ourselves, our parents, teachers, school, school mascot, world, town, city, color of the sky, taste of pears, air we breathe, and everything else we can and can't see. For ten (or fifty) years, we figure out what makes us tick—our likes, tolerances, and dislikes. We make friends, create enemies, remember nothing learned in the classroom, but feel every misplaced word pointed in our direction as a crime against humanity. During these years, our bodies change. Boys search desperately for facial hair (and pubic), girls search for bumps to become boobs, and all that matters is where the next pimple will make its next surprise appearance. It seems impossible at the time, but most of us get through it with only minimal mental scars and vivid memories of a girl's bra strap showing through her T-shirt two seats ahead and thinking, *There are boobs in there.* (I know I wasn't the only one.) What do you expect? For ten years, we're brain dead. We're walking zombies governed by hormones, gently moaning, "That's not fair. That's not fair," while sucking our teeth in disgust. The Fred Savage years are the worst years of our life, no exception. But for me, they meant finding out what it meant to be "black."

I don't mean black like, "Is she dark skinned like Rudy on *The Cosby Show*, or light skinned like Witly on *It's a Different World?*" but like, "You're black, so you can dunk, right?" *Black* meant how cool you were and, if you were a nerd, it was a question that came up every 2.3 seconds (like the bra strap). And although the question came and went over the years, there were two small but impressionable events that made me question my "blackness" above all the other name calling and tears that surfaced throughout the years.

The first was at my grandmother's house in York, Alabama.

Before I continue, I would like to paint a picture of this small Alabama town. Then, the town was Mayberry, if Mayberry had black people. It consisted of two gas stations (one right across from the other), a convenience store called The Log Cabin that sold the best Bomb Pops (a.k.a. red, white, and blue popsicles), and a Church's Fried Chicken. It was the kind of place where everyone waved when they saw you drive down the street because they figured, if you were there, they must know you or be related to you. People left their houses and cars unlocked and had no fear that, when they returned, everything would be in its place. It was a nice town, but boring beyond belief. Watching the grass grow was *actually* a pastime, along with watching the paint dry, kicking the can, and any other old school southern clichés you can think of. I can only assume that it's because of the boredom that my grandparents ended up having twelve children. You have to do something to pass the time.

The year was 1995. I was ten and at my grandparent's house known simply by everyone as "The Hill." Everyone called it "The Hill" because the one room shack my grandfather had built and pieced together into a fourteen-room house sat on top of a huge hill surrounded by about ten acres of farmland, pigs, forest, and a partial junkyard. It's where my grandmother farmed, my grandfather raised and slaughtered pigs, and my uncles and aunts worked on cars in their heyday. A few of them still sat in the yard and around the house collecting weeds, rust, dirt, and grass (the cars, not my aunts and uncles).

It was August and, after a twelve-hour drive, we were back for our annual weeklong supposed vacation/boring family visit.

It was morning and all my uncles and aunts had come to "The Hill" for breakfast. They sat at the kitchen table talking, laughing, and making fun of each other like they always did when they all came together. I was just waking up and moving from the back bedroom of the house to the kitchen when I heard one of my uncles say through the crack of the door separating the kitchen from the back rooms of the house, "Either Kenny's going to be gay when he grows up, or marry a white woman." Everyone laughed, clapped, and slapped their knee at its hilarity and how it wasn't, but was, but wasn't (but really was) true.

I don't remember if my mom or Aunt Jackie stuck up for me, but I do remember feeling pretty crappy, wondering why I wasn't "black" as I made my way to the bathroom rather than the kitchen. I didn't ask why they didn't *see* me as being "black", or why I didn't *feel* or *act* "black," but why I *wasn't* "black." The thought and feeling has yet to fully vanish. It's a thought that often comes when I'm around family. Hell, the first and only real words I remember my grandfather saying to or about me was, "If Kenny ever went and talked to a girl, he would say 'Hi,'" he pretended to take two puffs of an imaginary inhaler, "'you wanna go out?'" Everyone always laughs and calls these "jokes," but they are really a reflection of their version of the truth.

The second incident happened three years later. I was in eighth grade and loved to run, but was cursed with asthma (as my grandfather knew so well) any time I ran more than a block. I've had asthma all my life, but that was the first time I was able to get medication to treat my symptoms when they popped up. I had just come back from my first doctor's appointment and was very excited, giddy to say the least, with the new medication I had been given (Advair, Diskus, and Sinculair). I had gone to the bathroom skipping and singing, "A Whole New World" in preparation for the upcoming Children's Community Theatre audition (no joke), to read the directions and take my first dose of sweet savior, when I heard my sister say to Mom, "I've never seen someone so excited to take medicine before." I cried, my sister apologized, and everyone moved on, except for me. It didn't have quite the impact as my uncle implying that I wasn't "black", but it hurt more because it came from someone immediate. It implied I was different from other people like me and that I needed to behave "normally" in order to be socially accepted.

Both incidences made me not only wonder who I was (as the wonder years are supposed to do), but why I wasn't black, normal, and able to fit in.

In the nineties, and in many ways now, *black* was not a color, it was a way of being and behaving. In the mind of an adolescent black boy who always felt like an outsider, looking over the rim of his glasses toward the socialites, being black meant you had to prove your "blackness." This meant acting and looking *black*. So, in order to figure out how to fit in and be "more black," I created a mental checklist I needed to complete sometime before the end of my life in order to become as black as (if not blacker than) Shaft. I created this list after studying my brother (who I thought was the coolest person alive), TV shows, music videos, movies, friends, relatives, enemies that always seemed to take the girl I liked (I still hate you SJ), and what fragments of information I could get from the science fiction and fantasy books that occupied most of my time. The checklist went as follows.

Step 1: Basketball is the key! Every socially accepted black boy I had ever met knew how to play basketball. They played for a team, could shoot three-pointers and make layups, watched it on TV, but, more importantly, could dribble the ball between their legs. In my mind, this was the coolest thing in the world. It was modern magic to be able to move from bouncing a ball with one hand to bouncing it with the other through outstretched legs without it hitting you in the balls (as it always did with me). In my head, if I was going to be black, I had to play basketball. You didn't have to play football, but you had to know the rules, which I knew nothing about. I still don't.

Step 2: Look good, no matter what. Being black meant looking good all the time. Your hair was always cut and faded, and the clothes you bought were always new and brand-name (Nike Jordan, K-Swiss, Nautica, Tommy Hilfiger, Polo). This also meant you always looked cool. Whether it was sipping a can of soda, or walking down the driveway, you always looked cool. Words came out as smooth like the silk shirts I begged my mother to buy for me.

Step 3: Black girlfriend! This was the most difficult and the most important. Achieving step three would mean I had made it. I had to somehow, against all odds, be transformed from Steve Urkel to Stephon Arkel. Somehow, I had to be dowsed in a poorly-labeled container of toxic waste and emerge transformed into the new and improved, more powerful, more cool, more black, Super Junior; blacker, stronger, and more attractive than any adaptation of Shaft (Samuel L. Jackson, Micael Cira, or any other). It was only a dream because I had a weakness, like supercharged kryptonite, constantly working against me—the nerd checklist.

Step 1: Reading books was awesome! I loved books! I still love books, especially science fiction and fantasy. Reading a book a day in middle school for the Accelerated Reader Program was not cool. Writing short stories for the Young Author submission was not cool. I couldn't put the books away. As Pookie said in *New Jack City*, "They just keep callin' me, man. They just keep callin' me." No matter how hard I tried and how many new clothes I bought myself, I couldn't make reading a book look cool.

Step 2: Oops! If you've ever seen *The Goonies*, you know of Chunk. There's a scene in the movie in which all the kids are in the basement hiding from the Fratellis and looking for the secret entrance to One-Eyed-Willie's treasure, when Chunk starts yelling that they all need to leave. In the middle of his rant he runs into a watercooler, grabs the base, and tries to keep it from falling to the ground, but it's too late. It hits the floor, shatters into a million pieces, and in unison everyone says, "You klutz!" That, ladies and gentleman, was me trying to dribble a basketball down an empty court, let alone between my legs. It was impossible.

Step 3: I was ugly! On top of everything else, I was ugly. What I didn't know was that every middle school student is ugly. It's true, there are some gods and goddesses of middle school who are gorgeous, but they are few and far between. Everyone else looks up at Mount Olympus from far below and wonders what ambrosia tastes like. All normal middle schoolers have limbs out of proportion, zits that appear overnight, and smells wafting from orifices that secrete juices that you thought only appeared in D rated horror movies. It can't be helped. All anyone can do is keep breathing until high school, when you can get muscles and grow into your body. Until then, you're at the mercy of the preteen gods.

This was me. I was/am a nerd. There was nothing I could do to make myself more "black," so I gave in. I embraced it. I did what I liked rather than what was expected. I ran cross-country, became a drama geek, read books that weren't assigned, did speech and debate, and listened to Jason Mraz and John Mayer. I knew I wasn't behaving very *black*, but I was happy. Eventually, I stopped noticing the stares and the comments either because they went away or they didn't matter anymore. High school and college came and went, and, eventually, over time, I became me.

But this idea of "being black" stays with me nevertheless and still leaves me questioning, *Am I black enough?* And the answer is, no, I'm not, because "being black" doesn't matter when it compares to being a good husband and a good father.

My uncle was right, sort of. In his eyes, I did marry a white woman rather than a beautiful dark-skinned African queen, as they would say. However, in my eyes, I married my best friend—the college roommate with whom I shared an apartment while she was engaged to another man (that's an entirely different story for another time). I married the person with whom I knew I could spend the rest of my life and raise a family. I could be happy to laugh, cry, read, watch bad movies, and just sit around and do nothing with her until I die. I love my wife and the life we have built together. I love my children more than I could ever love myself. Everything I do and decide is for them. These things don't make me black, but they make me a good man, and that's something of which I am far more proud. Being black never meant loving Sarah any less, or dampening the pain of miscarrying our first child, even if I can't dribble a basketball between my legs. And if there's one thing I've learned from being in an inter-racial couple, it's that, no matter the skin color, love is colorless and the woman is always right.

Sleepover (Fiction)

"Do you think the world is going to end?"

She's already in bed, sheet pulled over her chest, arms at her side, looking at the ceiling. I pull off my shirt and throw it in the closet. These conversations always happen at weird times of the day or night—at one-thirty on a Saturday afternoon, or on six-hour car rides from Baltimore to Pittsburgh to see her family. They start with little questions like, "Do you think the world is going to end?" And the questions are gateways into deeper, more complicated fears she might be having about the development, or lack thereof, of her career; war; the migratory patterns of the slugs in Venezuela; the state of our sex life; or the social development of our unborn child (Amelia or Mark, we haven't decided. We only have two more years to figure it out if all goes according to plan. It never does.). Either way, I know the question means nothing. It's just the foreplay; the appetizer before the meat and potatoes of what's really on her mind. And I know what she wants me to say, but, for one reason or another, I always say the opposite.

"No."

Plain, simple, to the point—she hates it when I get to the point.

"How can you say that? You're the science fiction writer."

Oh boy, this is going to be a good one. Maria never brought up my writing. She hates my writing. She's never said that she hates my writing, but how could she? She's my wife.

"Yes I am," I say. "But I write it—I don't believe it. There's a reason they call it science fiction, not science fact. I'm a fiction writer. Do you believe every child can learn? You're the school teacher."

Now, she has two options. She can either (A) let it drop, roll over, and go to sleep, or (B) probe me for more information like an alien searching for farts. Option (C), which is no longer on the table, would be she rolls over, we make out, and spend the rest of the night having sex. Option (C) hasn't been on the table since we said, "I do" (things fathers-in-law tell you but you don't believe).

She watches the ceiling fan turn slowly above. The box it came in said that the blades are supposed to circulate the heat in the winter. I don't believe it. She still stares at the ceiling as I crawl into bed. Pulling the sheets back, I can see the outline of her pink sweatpants. Option (C) is definitely not on the table. If there is no possibility of sex, then there is no reason to end the conversation. My best bet is to remain aloof and make her slightly angry. It's the only way to get any sort of entertainment out of the night, and I already took a nap earlier in the day so there is no need to rush to bed. Like she said, I'm a science fiction writer. I get up when I want.

"You mean, you don't believe that one day all of this is going to end?" she asks. "That we, as a human race, are going to destroy ourselves?"

As you can already assume, she has chosen option (B).

Let me take this time to tell you a little about Maria. First, she's an eccentric. When something happens in the world, she is the tsunami that is the result of the beating of a butterfly's wings. A bomb goes off in Somalia and it changes what food

71

we buy and where we buy it, for at least a week. Oil spills off the coast, and we don't eat out for a month. To this day, I'm trying to convince her that we have nothing to fear from the Tea Party, but that's one ledge I think I'll join her on. So, when my wife asks me if the world is going to end, I know it has nothing to do with my writing. My best bet is to throw her a curve ball and see if she swings.

"It depends on what you mean."

She turns over on her side and looks me in the eyes. I have her attention. Or is it the other way around?

"Do you believe the world, the earth as a whole, is going to end? Do you believe we will, one day, hit the button and destroy ourselves in a nuclear war?"

"No."

"But do you believe our world, as we know it, is going to end one day?"

"Yes."

I can tell by the look on her face that she is eyeing the bait, questioning whether or not to take it.

"What do you mean?" she asks.

"The world we live in, our world, our reality, will one day no longer exist. The world of our grandparents has come to an end."

"What do you mean?"

Bait taken. Now I just have to reel her in.

"When they were young, our age or younger, they believed the world they lived in would last forever. They believed they could eat, drink, and smoke with no consequences because no one told them there were any. And if someone did, they didn't pay attention. Cars, homes, lives would remain the same forever. Our parents thought the same thing. Slightly different, but still in essence the same. Until, one day, the bubble burst and the world they knew no longer existed. The need for technology outweighed the necessity for convention. Health was no longer an issue, it was *the* issue. Medications and the need for happiness in the form of a pill became your God-given right. And the stability of everything, from the world economy to home ownership, became a question no one could answer. The world they knew, slowly but surely, came to an end—as will ours."

"What about now?"

"Now? The world is falling apart to be rebuilt. It's moving from autumn to winter, or spring to summer. It's in the middle of transition, and we're in limbo."

Sometimes, I even amaze myself. Where do I get this stuff? Probably an amalgamation of Saturday morning cartoons, good/bad eighties movies, *Full House*, and *Family Matters*. It may all seem out of place, but, in the end, it all fits together. Why? Because people want to believe. All that matters is presentation and timing. This is what she needs to hear at this moment, and the next thing out of her mouth will prove it. She stares into my eyes, taking in every word, and says, without missing a beat:

"Let's buy a house."

Bingo! The heart of the conversation. The main course of the meal. After two years of marriage, one year of engagement, and three years of on-again, off-again dating, I am getting good at this. Now, getting out unscathed is an entirely different issue. My best bet is to play it the same as usual until inspiration strikes.

"Maria—"

I feign amusement tinged with slight annoyance.

"Hear me out."

She grabs my chest and pleads for me to listen. Now, I stare into the ceiling fan. It's all a performance. This should be one of the first lessons men learn. Unfortunately, it's usually the last.

"Listen. We can use my teacher discount. If we buy a house in the city, we can get tax rebates and financial assistance through the GNP. All we have to do is—"

"Take out a loan we won't get approved for."

Her face drops.

"Maria, we don't have the money." I turn towards her. "Not yet. But we will."

She stares. I stare. In her eyes, I see that I've won, or so I think.

Gentlemen, in every argument there are two sides. And I'm not talking about a right and a wrong side, or a *his* side and a *her* side. In an argument between lovers, there is a logical side and an emotional side. Throughout the years, I have become a master of the logical equation of persuasive rhetoric. Unfortunately, I have had little practice in emotion, which my wife has fluently exercised since the day she first drew breath into her tiny baby lungs and began to cry. No matter how I study and practice logic, my Kung Fu is no match for hers. However, true masters can weave the two sides of the equation evenly together and bring balance to the force. I have yet to meet one so powerful.

"Wait one, maybe two more years, and everything will fall into place," I say. "We'll have enough for a down payment, better credit, and we'll be able to start having kids. That's the plan, right? One to two years."

"Yeah," she says, "but I want to start now."

I apologize. My wife isn't nearly this whiney. She may be a queen of emotional argument, but she isn't annoying about it. Let me try that line again.

"Yeah," she says, "that's the plan."

Much better.

"But," she asks, "do you know how old my parents were when they bought their first house?"

She turns on to her stomach and speaks into the wall. I stay on my side.

"Twenty-four! Twenty-four and they were on their way to owning their own house. I'm thirty—"

"Twenty-eight."

"But I'm going to be thirty."

"Didn't we agree you weren't going to say you were thirty until you were *actually* thirty?"

"I'm twenty-eight. In two years, I'll be thirty, then forty. And we still haven't even started a family. I hate to think what everyone is going to say about me."

This last statement is made more to herself than to me. She turns on her stomach and continues the argument of emotion as I lie with my head in my hands, staring and compiling my counter argument.

"They say," she explains more to herself than to me, "Maria's only a teacher—not a mom. She's finally working after starting her career two years out of college, but she still hasn't bought a house. When is she going to start having kids? Maybe she can't. Maybe they don't want to have kids. They are *different*."

Opportunity!

"Who says that? No one says *different*."

I turn over onto my stomach, too.

"No, but they could."

Counter argument.

"Let's look at the whole picture before we start to get hysterical and freak out about the future. First, how much was your parent's first house?"

I saw myself as Perry Mason or Matlock, walking from one side of the courtroom to the other as a jury watched my every move and hung on to my every word.

"That doesn't matter. What matters is—"

"How much?"

"I can't remember."

"How much, Maria?"

"Fifty-two thousand dollars."

"What kind of house can you buy now, in the city, for fifty-two thousand dollars?"

"I don't—"

"None that's still standing." She sits silently. Logic begins to win. "Second, how old was your mom when she got married?"

She's reluctant, but answers.

"Twenty-two. Two years younger than me when I got married."

First and most important rule of engagement – never ask a question you don't already know the answer to.

"Yes, but how old was she when she had your sister?"

Trap set and sprung.

"Nineteen, but—"

"But the point is she had your sister at nineteen, got married at twenty-two, and put the down payment for their first house at twenty-six. You and I married at twenty-four, after getting our degrees, and making sure we have more of what we need to start a family rather than just figuring it out as we go. What did I tell you while planning the wedding?"

She thinks a minute without responding. This is the part of the argument where attack is no longer needed. To make sure I don't sleep on the couch, or freeze from lack of sheets on my side of the bed, I have to rebuild and make her not feel so bad for losing the argument.

"I said there was no set plan, except the one we made for ourselves. Just because someone did it before, it doesn't mean we can't do it differently. Everyone writes their own story."

That was in my fortune cookie at dinner the night before. Every experience is a learning opportunity (that's a fortune too).

She stares into the pillow. I can tell she is realizing the truth of everything I said. This is the point when she acknowledges I've won, rolls over, and thanks me for keeping her grounded.

That is, if the argument were over. I should know better; the argument is never over.

She rolls on her back, stares into the ceiling fan and asks, "Do you remember when we met?"

"Yes," I say, unsure of how that fits into the conversation. "Which time? When we were just friends, or when I moved in with you and your roommate."

"Or the time you attacked me when we first kissed?" she says with a smile.

"I did not attack you," I say, turning over.

"You nearly swallowed my face."

"I couldn't help it. You can't make a person wait three years to date, and then not expect a little excitement when making first contact."

Time for a history lesson. Maria and I met during my sophomore year in college, one cold Saturday morning in February before boarding a van with twelve other young adults in suits. We were all on our way to a speech and debate tournament, and Maria was one of the new members of the team. I could attempt to make college students giving up their weekends to put on suits and deliver ten-minute memorized speeches sound cool, but there is no way I could makes us sound better than glorified band geeks. She had a container of baked muffins and wore a pencil skirt that is burned into my memory. On that morning in February, I fell in love with my wife, even if she doesn't believe me. I guess I don't blame her since I said nothing to her that entire day, or the following week for that matter. But, we ended up becoming good friends—best friends actually. And we stayed best friends for three years because it took that long for her and her fiancé to break up.

Now, I know what you're thinking: I split them up. But that's not true. I loved Mathew. I loved them so much, I moved in with them. That's right, I moved in with my future wife and her fiancé. It sounds weird, doesn't it? Just know that Maria and I did nothing wrong while we were all living together. We were best friends, even though I wanted more. Nothing happened until the third year of our friendship.

Maria was living alone. Mathew moved away for graduate school. They had been having problems for a while and agreed, mutually, to break up. I had nothing to do with it. I was going through my own problems with my long-term girlfriend that I also broke up with on the same day as her and Matt. Anyway, hearing the news, I offered to come over and make her my famous spaghetti stew. Before I knew it, one thing lead to another, and I was attacking her with my lips. I literally attacked her. I had been waiting for that kiss for three years; what else was I supposed to do. As they say, the rest is history.

I lie there, smiling to myself, thinking about our history and remembering everything we put each other through over the years, when she asks:

"If we had never started dating, and never got married, where do you think you would be now?"

"Besides the University of Alaska?"

"You never would have gone."

I smile.

"The truth is, I've never thought about it." I sit and think for a minute. "I don't know. Where would you be?"

She doesn't miss a beat.

"Probably teaching English in South Korea."

She doesn't look at me to gauge my reaction. Either she already knows or doesn't care.

"If I never came over after you and Mathew broke up and fixed you spaghetti stew and made out with you on your broken futon, you would be in Korea teaching English rather than in Pittsburgh?"

"Yup. Want to know how I'd have ended up there?"

She dangles the bait in front of me on a silver platter. My defenses are completely down. I know what is happening, but I can't stop my inevitable downfall, like a mosquito is drawn to the irresistible light of a bug zapper.

The first and most important rule is never ask a question to which you don't already know the answer. She knows what I will say.

"Sure. How?"

"Well, if you never came over, and we never started going out, I would have dated, a lot!" she says looking directly in my eyes to make sure I completely understand what she means. It twists the knife a little deeper. "Do you remember how much sex we had those first few weeks? I would have had to get that fulfilled by someone. It was just your luck that it was you. It could have been anyone, or any more than one. Being in a long term relationship for three years with a fiancé who hardly ever wants to have sex really makes a girl needy, and a little desperate."

I'm not sure if my face shows the anger and heartbreak I feel toward all the imaginary men she never slept with, but she either didn't notice or didn't care.

"I would have continued to fool around with a few guys in my program, or random men I met at the club, until I finished my master's, applied to the teaching program in Korea, and never looked back."

Trap set and sprung.

She knows my thoughts. She knows the random faces of strange men I picture hitting on my wife in countless bars, buying countless drinks, telling silly jokes that make no sense before taking her back to their apartment, or going to hers, to do things on that broken futon I won't mention here. I hate these men. I want to rip out their larynxes with my fingertips, like Patrick Swayze in *Roadhouse*, and watch them drop lifelessly into a still lake. And she knows it.

Now, this is the part in the argument when attack is no longer needed.

She rolls over, kisses me on my lips and says, "Best sleepover ever," before turning out the light and going to sleep.

Logic is no competition for emotion. Its Kung Fu is too strong.

MALE

"The superior man is distressed by the limitations of his ability; he is not distressed by the fact that men do not recognize the ability that he has." – Confucius

Frankenstein's Monster

The only problem I have with growing old is smelling more and more like my father. As a kid, there was nothing more disgusting, potent, and loud than my father's farts. Their roar and stench filled every inch of the room. There was no escape. How bad were they? Imagine taking a gallon of milk, leaving it in the trunk of a ninety-three Ford Taurus during the hottest week of August, along with twelve dozen eggs, five bags of onions, and a packet of catfish fillets with all the ingredients to make mom's delicious after-church spaghetti. Now imagine opening the gallon of milk while being trapped in the trunk of that Ford Taurus with the rust spots on the undercarriage. That is what it was like being in the room when my dad convinced one of us to "pull his finger." And that's what I'm beginning to smell like. The transformation can't be reversed.

This is me now. Since high school, college, and my twenties, I've changed. In the past, the problems I had with my father and mother and the life we lived were much more real and life altering. Then, the only way I could come to grips with reality without going insane was with pen and paper. This is reflected in the novella "Michael" that I wrote and published in my book of short stories, *Thoughts in Italics,* seven years ago.

Michael (Fiction)

"Hello, Michael."

Without turning, he already knew who it was. He had heard the voice only once before. But it came from the one person he had been expecting to see for many years and knew he would meet again . . . one day.

"Hello, Bastian."

Michael looked out over the lake he had called home for the past twenty years and marveled at the sunset. Not because he knew that it would be the last he would ever see, but because, in the twenty years he had been sitting in his rocking chair with nothing but the sound of the wind and the crickets to keep him company, he had never seen the same sunset twice. If it were up to him, he would never let the sun go down.

Bastian stepped forward and stood beside Michael, watching the silent ending of another day. Michael looked up and saw that Bastian had not aged a day since the last time they had met, seventy-five years ago. He even wore the same clothes. This did not surprise Michael. He smiled, turned his head, and continued to watch the setting sun.

"You haven't changed."

"But you have. Time has changed you for the better because of the worst." Michael knew this to be true. It was during many of those "worst" moments in his life that he had hated Bastian the most.

"Would you like to go in? We can talk more comfortably inside," said Michael.

"Yes. That would be fine."

Michael grabbed the cane that rested on the side of his chair and, with a strain, forced himself to get up. Bastian took his other hand and helped him to his feet.

"Thank you." Bastian simply smiled, following the old man into the cabin. Michael made his way to a cushioned seat in the living room, beside a small table that held a lamp and a copy of *Paradise Lost*.

"Still haven't finished it yet, eh?" Bastian asked with a smile.

"It's worth re-reading." Michael spoke slowly and with a slight rasp to his voice, as he let gravity take control of his body and sit him down with a thump and a loss of breath.

"Would you like something to drink?" Bastian asked.

"Water, please."

Bastian stepped into the kitchen and filled two coffee cups with water from the faucet; Michael liked it better that way. For some odd reason, he thought it tasted better. Bastian couldn't help smiling to himself as he remembered this small detail among countless others. He knew everything there was to know about Michael without actually knowing Michael. For so many years, Bastian had watched him from a distance, even in those private moments when Michael believed no one else was watching. But he had only talked to him once, and then only for a brief moment. Bastian often wondered what was going through Michael's mind.

After giving Michael his cup of water, Bastian went to the chair on the other side of the room and sat down. Michael took a few sips, set the cup down on the table beside him, and looked up at the old friend sitting across from him.

"Is it that time already?"

"I think you know the answer."

"What am I supposed to do?"

"Nothing. For the time being. For now, I just want to talk with you."

"About what?"

"About your life. About what you've learned, and whether you believe it was worth it."

Michael sat silently in his chair and wondered how to explain the scope of his life in a conversation. It was filled with so much. Much of it too great for words.

"I can't put my entire life into words. I've lived through too much, been too many places, met too many people. Most of the years and incidents have blended together into a kaleidoscope of memories, dreams, and reality. I wouldn't know what to talk about."

"You don't have to tell me everything. I was there for all of it. Just tell me what you remember the most. What do you often look back on? What had the greatest impact on the way you lived and viewed your life?"

Michael thought it over for a moment and said, "Okay. Where would you like me to start?"

"Where would you like to start?"

Michael sat silently, then began. "As I've gotten older, I find myself looking to the beginning of my life more and more. Never looking for answers, but always finding them. The more I look back, the more I understand myself. I've forgotten most of my life, but I remember the beginning and what it taught me. So I'll tell you about the first quarter of my life."

"The beginning it is."

Michael took another sip of his water and began to think over the first words to say. The sun had stopped setting and remained motionless in the sky, just as Michael had hoped it would. Time had come to a pause.

Michael put down his cup of water again and opened his mouth to speak, but was cut short. Before a single word could pass his lips, Bastian interjected.

"Actually, do you mind if I begin? I believe that there are a few things about your life that you are not aware of. Certain things about your birth that even your parents didn't know."

Michael nodded his head in agreement and wondered what new information Bastian had to offer.

"As you may have already figured out, we were there the day you were born—a few of the nurses, a doctor, a patient being admitted into the emergency room. We were scattered throughout the hospital. All of us were on edge, waiting to hear news of you. Some of us also had other business at the hospital, but many of us were just there to await your arrival and make sure there were no complications with the labor. We watched as your mother came into the hospital, and waited throughout the labor for your arrival. Your birth caused her no pain. She did not scream. The labor was short, and when you finally came into the world, and breathed in your first breath of air, the electricity in the room went out. When you exhaled the lights came back on, and you were in the hands of the doctor. Your eyes were closed and you were not crying. All eyes were silently on you. As if you knew you were being watched, you opened your eyes and looked around the room at the strange faces. No one spoke a word, but everyone marveled at the beauty of your eyes that reminded them of an autumn day. Some colors were blended together and others stood out vividly. After all these years, your eyes have remained the same. You did not cry as they cut your umbilical cord, cleaned you off, and gave you to your mother. And as your mother took you in her arms and looked deep into your eyes for the very first time, you smiled and stole the breath of everyone in the room. That was the first time I saw you."

"Bastian, why are we doing this?"

"I told you, I just wanted to hear how you viewed your life."

"Yes, but everything I can say, you already know. You were there every day of my life. I never saw you, but I knew you were watching, guarding, protecting. I could feel your presence and knew you were close, but you never interfered. Even when I needed your help the most, you never gave me any. I even called on you, but you never appeared—except once before now. And that is only because you were told to meet me."

Michael was not angry. There was nothing he could do to change the past, so there was no need to get angry over what could have been. Bastian smiled from across the table and simply said, "I had orders."

"I know you did. I know. But why are we talking about my life? Is this another order that was given to you?"

"No. This is simply me being curious. Besides, when all this is over, I won't remember anything about what took place during these past ninety-eight years."

Michael had forgotten that.

"Very well then. I'll tell you what I remember most about my life and what I held most dear if you promise me one thing."

"What would that be?"

"You tell me, truthfully, if at some point during my life, I received help in any way from you or anyone else."

Bastian sat quietly for a moment and finally agreed.

"Excellent. Now where to begin? How about where you left off? My childhood."

"Sounds good."

"There are few things from my childhood that I can remember actually happening. Much of it has either been forgotten or confused with a dream. I am not sure if my first memory is my own or the imprint of a photograph that I saw as a child. The only thing that remains definite throughout all these years are the emotions I felt. As a child, all of them seemed to be more genuine. When I was sad, it seemed to make all the sense in the world for me to feel that way. My tears fell from the creases in my eyes, and I never held them back. They flowed as free as a faucet. My joy knew no bounds. I remember not always smiling, but feeling happy, and never having any regrets. My fears where of actual things, not of the unexpected days that lay ahead. My feelings defined who I was. Not the clothes I wore, or the job I had. My universe rotated around the life I lived inside my house on 2037 North Woodrow Drive. The coming of a new day never filled me with worry, stress, and melancholy. Instead, it felt as if I would live forever.

"When did these feelings stop? For most, the change is so gradual that they never see it taking place. But I did. I saw it, and I tried desperately to hold on to the past. I tried to hold on to the boy that I used to be—a boy who still saw joy in the world and knew all the answers to whatever life threw at me. Unfortunately, like everyone else, I lost the battle and became an adult. But I never fully grew up. I still hold on to that little six-year-old boy that would daydream in his back yard for hours and never wonder what time of day it was.

"It's true that I grew up into the old man that you see sitting before you, but I'm the man I am today because of the teachers I had throughout my life. Now, let me clarify. When I say teachers, I don't just mean school teachers, but anyone, or anything, that I came into contact with that could teach me a lesson, good or bad.

"The first people I remember teaching me the valuable and long lasting lessons were my neighbors. But they were not just my neighbors. They were also my babysitters and basically like my grandparents. They kept me when no one was home; they picked me up from elementary school every day that my mom was not off from work. My school was on the road across the street from my house, so one of them would always meet me at the crosswalk and walk me back to their house. Most of the time it was Roy. Their names were Roy and Miss Della Jones. Roy would always crack jokes and play with me, while Miss Della had more of a strict, but loving, hand. She taught me the value of manners and morals.

"I remember the first time I stayed at her house. She told me that I would not get anything in her house without saying yes ma'am, no ma'am, yes sir, or no sir. She said that you have to respect your elders and do as they tell you. I listened to the words she spoke to me and saw no signs of a smile on her face. I feared her, but knew she would never hurt me. Instead, I wanted to show her that I could follow her rules and treat her with the respect she demanded. I soon learned that by treating others with respect, you get it in return.

"I never played with toys when I went to Roy and Miss Della's house. Instead, I would sit on their couch and watch whatever was on their television if I wasn't doing my homework. In all my years there, there was one thing that never changed. Every day, after school, Miss Della would fix me a bowl of chicken noodle soup and a cup of juice. That's what I always wanted, and that is what she always fixed."

Michael paused for a moment and smiled to himself before resuming.

"This took place throughout elementary school. I loved Roy and Miss Della as if they were my family. To me they were my grandparents. When Grandparents Day came around at school, I asked Roy to be my grandfather for the day, and he happily accepted. He and I would always get on each other's case. He would get on me for being young and I would get on him for being old. He was a great friend who could always put a smile on my face. They taught me the difference between right and wrong; and, in many cases, they taught me friendship. They were hard at times, but always loving. My family was good at bringing me up as best they could, but Roy and Miss Della filled in the gaps. They provided an understanding that only someone much older than myself could give about the way to live a good life. I owe to them the humility, respect, and manners I carry with me as a man today. I would have paid them back, and told them all this, but I never got the chance."

He had to pause. He knew what he was going to say, but it hurt him to bring back the final memories he had of them. He knew of the good times, and spoke of them with ease, but he did not want to speak or remember the bad. Bastian said nothing while he waited for Michael to begin again. He looked at Michael, who stared at the floor, gathering strength for the words he spoke next.

"At the beginning of my freshman year in high school, I was told by my mother that Miss Della had been diagnosed with breast cancer. Miss Della had known for a while, but had kept it to herself. She saw no reason to cause anyone else to worry. But my mother now knew because Miss Della was going on chemotherapy and had told her of the situation. She didn't want us to worry when we saw that she wasn't getting around like her old self. The doctors believed she would pull through. There was no reason for me to have a babysitter anymore, but I still went by and visited when I could. I still joked around with Roy and told Miss Della how I was getting along. But she had little to no energy, and most of her hair was gone. By the end of my freshman year, all of her hair had fallen out. But she was recovering."

Michael's eyes began to glisten with the approach of a tear as clouds began to gather outside the cabin. It looked like it was going to rain, but it didn't. Michael held back his tears and continued.

"Most of her energy had returned, but only for a short while. The chemo was complete, and all of the cancer had been removed, but it had damaged her body in the process. It had weakened her to the point where her body could not function until she finally died. Roy died about six months later. He had nothing left in the world to keep him going. I think about them sometimes, and how much they shaped me."

Bastian sat quietly on the other side of the room as he listened to Michael's last words. As he spoke them, the clouds began to clear and the sun began to shine again from its halted spot in the heavens. The room remained quiet as the sun shone brightly through the kitchen window.

Michael stared off into nothing. He wasn't sure where to begin next, so he sat patiently, waiting for Bastian to speak.

"Is there something else you would like to tell me?" Michael asked.

"About what?

Michael looked at Bastian and said nothing. He knew Bastian would tell him, and he did.

"Yes. They were two of us," Bastian admitted. "Did you know?"

"I had my assumptions. They taught me so much I thought they may have had a larger part in this then I realized."

"Does it make you love them any less?"

"Not at all."

"You don't feel as if the lessons they taught you were false?"

"Not in the least. The lessons they taught me were genuine and from the heart. They loved me and nothing can change that. And for that I will always love them."

Bastian paused, looked into Michael's eyes for a moment, and smiled. Michael continued the story of his life.

"You spoke of your neighbors before you gave any thought to your mother, father, sister, or brother."

"I did think of them, but I didn't want to speak of them first because it seemed as though they were not the first to have such a major impact on my life."

"And you feel the Joneses did?"

Michael thought for a moment and answered, "Yes, I do."

Bastian said nothing.

"This does not mean my family did not have any input into the man I am today, and the views I carry with me. In fact, I remember their lessons much more vividly, and I cherish them much more than the time I spent with the Joneses or anyone else. Each one of them, in their own way, molded. They shaped me because I looked up to them and didn't want to disappoint them. They represented my first exposure to truth, honesty, love, and compassion.

"I know that my family is no different from countless others, and it may seem that they are not special—but they are. All families provide the basic building blocks for a developing human. But not all of them are good. I was just lucky enough to be given such a great family. They have been a part of my life since the day I was born, and they will stay a part of my life until the day I die, even if they have all passed away.

This is what Bastian wanted. He had seen all of Michael's life from a distance, but he didn't understand the concepts that drove him to act the way he did. He never fully understood how you could have a connection with people that you did not always get along with. Michael's family argued, got angry at one another, and wouldn't talk for months and sometimes years at a time. But whenever one of them was sick or in so much trouble that they didn't know where to turn, they were always there to support each other. He admired the family, but never fully understood it. This was his chance.

"But you didn't always like the people in your family. In fact, at one point you hated a few of them. So why do you still honor their memory with so much joy?"

Michael smiled.

"It is true, I did not always like my family, but I always loved them."

"I don't understand."

"I know it makes hardly any sense, but that's the whole point of having a family. They can drive you so crazy, and make you so mad that you wish they would drop off the face of the earth. But you know that no matter what is said between you, no matter how many arguments or hateful words you exchange, you always have someone you can turn to when things get bad and when fortune smiles. Friends can let you down, and often do, but family is there when you absolutely need them. They love you no matter what, and you love them because you know who they are, were, and can be. You know they are good people because you remember the good times you shared with them. And you hold on to the memory of those good times when things get tough, hoping that more days like them will come soon."

With each word Michael spoke, the sun that had paused in its descent from the heavens began to pulsate with an intense brightness. It blinded the sky into a pure white light that could only create amazement, not pain. As his words came to an end, the light faded to its normal intensity, the sky changed back into the blue, orange, and purple of a sunset, and Bastian looked at Michael in wonder and awe. Bastian did not speak, but he now understood.

"Would you like me to tell you about them?"

It took a moment for Bastian to answer. He gave a small smile back to Michael and said, "Yes, please."

"The story of each member of my family is different. Each of them gave me something different to learn from and to love.

"As you know, I had a brother and a sister, both of whom were older than me—my brother by ten years, and my sister by five. To me, we had the perfect age difference. I was able to hear from them about both middle school and high school. I had no fear because they had given me little hints on how to stay ahead of the game. It just seemed to work out. I remember the time I spent with my brother most vividly.

"My brother, Kevin, taught me the meaning of the word *cool*." Michael laughed to himself as he remembered the way he looked up to his brother and wanted to be just like him.

"Kevin always let me tag along. I hardly ever spoke when I was out with him and his friends, but I cherished every moment of it. Kevin was always involved in some kind of after school activity, mostly sports—track, wrestling, cross-country. He did almost anything that dealt with endurance and that gave him an excuse to get out of the house. He and my dad didn't always get along, but that's another story.

"As you already know, he was popular. When I was in grade school and he was in high school, it seemed like he knew everyone and everyone knew him—not only knew him, but liked him. He had great guy friends that he laughed and joked around with when they went to football and basketball games and gorgeous female friends that would always flirt with him. Of course, to a six-year-old boy, any girl over thirteen was worth dating. But it wasn't just because Kevin had friends that I looked up to him so much, it was because of his attitude. He treated everyone he met with respect. Of course, he would joke around about the way some people looked, or acted, but he was never rude. In a way, he taught me how to be chivalrous. He knew what was needed to keep balance in his life, and he passed the knowledge on to me, whether he knew it or not. To put it simply, he had a good soul, and he was a good man."

Michael paused for a moment, remembering his brother and smiling to himself.

"I have one memory that has stuck with me the most over all these years. It's when my brother was still living at home, and we shared a room. We had this little thirteen channel, twelve-inch TV that didn't get cable. Every night, my brother and I would watch Star Trek and the Late Night Show. What's funny is that I would almost never make it through Star Trek. But I always wanted to stay up for the Late Night Show. So, every night, I would ask my brother to wake me up if I fell asleep. He rarely did. And when he tried, I would never get up. But sometimes I would make it through Star Trek, or wake up in the middle of the Late Night Show and enjoy the two hours I got to spend alone with my big brother."

Michael smiled to himself again, enjoying the only thing that was left of his brother, his memory. The smile slowly faded, as time passed within his own mind, and he witnessed the circumstance that led up to his brother's abrupt departure from his childhood home.

"My sister, Michelle, was my arch enemy when I was younger." Both Michael and Bastian had to laugh at that, remembering how the siblings had tortured each other when they were children.

"What can I say about Michelle? There's not that much too say. We didn't start to get along until after my brother left. For a while she filled the gap he had left. I had always been a shy kid, at least up until high school. By sitting back and listening to the advice she gave me, and watching the way she interacted with her friends, she taught me how to fit in—and not just with one specific set of people. Michelle knew different kinds of people, and she was able to adjust to each of their personalities. She was friends with the cheerleaders, the jocks, the band and orchestra members, the preps, the spirit crew, the rebels, and the class clowns—anyone and everyone. She was a chameleon, able to fit in with any group of people in any circumstance. Kevin had friends, but he was never as charming and loved as Michelle.

"So many people liked her because she was always able to relate to something about the people she was around, whether that was through a song, a school activity, a show on TV, or a teacher that they both despised. She was able to figure out what the other person loved and show her interest in it. It was an art that I could never master the way she did. She was a genuine person who cared for the friends that she had no matter their background or skin color. The love she had for them showed in her words and her actions. That's why everyone loved her so much., not because they had something in common, but because she cared for them and so they cared for her back, just as I did.

"Kevin and Michelle taught me two very important, but different, things. Kevin taught me how to be debonair, cool, cultured, and sophisticated while still remaining a gentleman. Michelle showed me how to see the similarities I shared with other people, and how to relate to them. But she also taught me to learn from their differences so that I could grow as a person, and understand other frames of mind. My brother taught me how to wear the armor of a knight, while my sister taught me how to be the hero inside. Both aspects are key to my development into the old man you see and the way that I lived my life."

"I can tell that you really loved them."

"Yes, I did. However, as you know, we didn't always get along. As I grew up, things changed. We changed. And incidents happened that affected us all for the worse and took years to fix, but never fully. The scar always remained."

Bastian knew what he was speaking of, but he could tell that Michael wanted to talk about it.

"Tell me what happened."

"Soon, but first my parents. Every good story has a villain, except this one. There are no bad people. No one is plotting diabolical schemes to prove their superiority over anyone or anything else. No one is evil, but everyone is a teacher – you just have to know what lessons to take from them. I learned this many years ago from my father, not because he ever told it to me, but because he was a walking, talking, living example of how not to live my life and treat other people.

"The man that you see sitting across from you, Bastian, exists only because of my father. He taught me almost everything that I know about the kind of person I wanted to be. His methods were flawless."

"Wait, you are saying that you learned how to be a good person from the bad things your father did?" Bastian asked.

"Yes."

"So the generosity I've seen you display over the years—the compassion, the friendship, the meekness—everything that seems to represent your good nature is because of the evil in your father."

"Not evil, Bastian. My father was never evil. And he wasn't a bad man. He was just . . . mixed up."

Bastian didn't understand how Michael could still be defending his father after everything that he had put him through. Michael continued.

"My dad suffered from the same single-mindedness that afflicts most people. He saw the world through his eyes only. He never saw a circumstance from the perspective of another person. It is because of him that I think too deeply about how I may be ill-treating another person."

Bastian looked confused.

"Let me explain. I watched my father for years. He opened my eyes to how one person can make so many other people's lives miserable by looking out only for himself. And I listened to the complaints of the rest of my family about his attitude, taking it all in. I watched his rudeness, and how angry it made the people around him—it taught me how not to talk to someone. I saw the way he sometimes used fear and intimidation to scare the rest of the family into doing what he wanted, and so learned humility and meekness. I listened to his negligence of the things that people cared the most for in their lives, and learned how to listen to others and not simply wait for my turn to speak. The list is endless. When I took all that in, I gained more friends, trust, and respect then he did. He showed me all this not by telling me what to do right, but by showing me what to do wrong."

Bastian was finally starting to understand, but he saw a flaw in Michael's methods.

"He also scared you."

"What?" Michael didn't know what to say or how to react. It's true he didn't have the best father in the world, but he didn't feel as if he had ever been scared by him. "How so?"

"I noticed it a long time ago, after the incident with your brother. After he left, and your father was taking you and your family through so many changes, you realized you couldn't trust anyone. You felt as if the only person you could truly count on was yourself. I could see it every day in the way you took care of yourself. You rarely asked for help, but always offered your hand to friends in need. You felt that anyone you loved would eventually let you down, and so you had to prepare for the worst. You lived by this code faithfully your entire life, especially when your sister went away to college, leaving you to deal with a broken home by yourself."

Michael didn't know what to say. He kept thinking back to the night his brother was kicked out of the house. He replayed it over and over in his mind. With each flash of his memories, a new shadow appeared in the living room, and voices he hadn't heard for years echoed through the cabin.

He remembered only seeing shadows, and so that is what he saw play out in the middle of the living room between him and Bastian. It was the middle of the night, and Michael had been woken from his sleep by a yell from his mother. As his eyes focused, he looked into the hallway from the top of his bunk bed to see the shadow of his brother, a scrawny high school kid, lift, by the throat, his father who outweighed him by at least 120 pounds. Michelle was screaming from her room across from his own. He was in awe of what was taking place before his eyes, and afraid of what it meant.

Kevin couldn't hold a man of that size by the throat for long. His father broke free from Kevin's grip and punched him across the face, knocking him to the ground. After a few seconds, Kevin regained his composure, stood up, and was about to tackle his father. But his mother stood between them and held him back. Kevin told her to move, and she told him to leave. He said he wasn't going anywhere, but she told him to go out and cool off before he did anything stupid. Rather than seeing this as a mother trying to keep her family together, Kevin saw it as her taking the side of her husband. This made him even angrier, but he did as his mother told him to do— only he didn't come back. Michael watched from his top bunk as his brother grabbed a few changes of clothes beneath him, put them in his book bag, and walked out the door without saying good-bye.

With the sound of the front door slamming, the shadows slowly faded away, until he could only see Bastian sitting across from him.

"Everything went downhill after that. I still haven't fully recovered from that night. I watched the two greatest heroes I had ever known do battle. Superman and Batman were in a fist fight that cracked the foundations of my entire perspective of reality. The world was no longer as good as I had once made it out to be, and there was no going back to my childhood innocence. It's true that I saw a lot of flaws in my father's character, but I still looked up to him. He was my dad. But after that . . . after that, I never looked at him the same. And by brother went off to join the military and moved as far away from us as possible. He rarely wrote or called. Nothing was the same anymore, and it never would be again."

"Do you remember what the fight was about?" Bastian asked.

"A pillow. A stupid pillow. My father had forgotten his pillow on the basement couch and so he asked my mother for hers. She wouldn't give it to him, or go down and get his, so he pushed her out of bed. When she fell, she hit her head on the bedside table. Kevin was still awake and heard the entire thing. He went in to break up the argument, and my father got mad and pushed Kevin. The fact that his mom was on the floor holding her head and his adopted father was yelling and pushing him out of the room made Kevin angry enough to do what he did."

"That's right, you and your sister had a different dad than your brother."

"Yes, and that's why they hardly ever got along."

Bastian nodded his head in understanding, and Michael felt sadness for what took place that night and his inability to stop any of it from happening.

"You see, even though your father was your greatest teacher, he also gave you the greatest handicap—an inability to trust."

Michael sat silently and knew that Bastian was right. He knew his life was much more complex than the simple stories he was telling. There were good times, bad times, and people that hurt him. He didn't know how to explain it all. It was too big to be fully understood. He didn't know what to say next.

"Don't feel discouraged," Bastian said. "I simply did what you did. I watched and I learned. That is one of the things I learned from your life by watching it all these years. If you are involved in someone else's life, you are going to affect them for good and bad, no matter what."

Michael recognized the truth in what Bastian was saying. He was right. Bastian had always given him the truth . . . or so he believed. He thought back to that day at the coffee shop when they first met, and the message Bastian gave him that changed his life forever.

"So I take it that's how you knew I was coming."

"What do you mean?" asked Michael.

"Your abilities. The power you now have to make things happen by just thinking about them—the sunset, the sky, the replay of past memories as if they were happening for the first time was all under your control. You, Michael, are controlling all this."

"I know, but I don't know how I'm doing it. This all just started when you showed up a few hours ago. It seems that whatever I really want to happen, happens. I know you said this would happen, but you never said exactly when, how much power I would have, or how I would be able to control it."

"I didn't tell you because I didn't know. All of this is new to me as well. I just told you what I was told to tell you. I knew only enough to pass the truth along to you."

The day he met Bastian had always stayed on his mind. After that day, his life changed forever. How could it not? He was told truths he did not want to hear, and did not believe, but came eventually to accept.

"Do you remember that day?" Bastian asked.

"Of course I do. The memory is so fresh in my mind, I feel as if it happened yesterday. My mind always wonders back to that afternoon in the coffee shop and how different my life might have been if I had never met you."

And with those words the room, the cabin, the lake, everything vanished except Michael, Bastian, and the seats they sat in. The darkness blinded them from seeing even a hand's length in front of their faces. Nothing could be seen until lights appeared from overhead, and the sun shone in from a nearby glass door displaying a steaming coffee cup logo.

Jazz music played from a small speaker above as the stranger stood over a small, round café table. He looked down to see a half-finished cup of cold coffee, an ignored copy of *Paradise Lost* sprawled out on the table, and a handsome, slightly boyish young man sitting across from an empty seat. The young man's attention was focused on an empty maroon wall. The stranger looked up from the table to the wall, found nothing of any interest to keep his attention, and realized that, like a projector screen, the wall was playing out the scenes of dreams and sadness that occupied this young man's mind. The knowledge of knowing enough about the world to be afraid of it caused the young man to get lost inside his own thoughts for hours. But like a kid in a candy store, he could not focus on just one thought. His mind wondered from thought to thought, weighing each possibility for his future. He wanted it all, but he knew that was impossible.

The stranger smiled at the innocence that could still be seen in this young man and admired his ability to preserve it. The thoughts continued to circulate inside the young man's mind, and the stranger waited for his presence to be noticed. Then, with no invitation, the stranger moved to the opposite end of the table, picked up the chair, pulled it back, and sat down.

The young man swam back to the surface of reality with a start and a look of confusion. The stranger adjusted himself in his seat and smiled back at the young man's bewildered gaze. Staring at the stranger, the young man attempted to figure out this intruder. The white collared shirt and black peat coat offered no explanation, but still he felt an odd attraction to this man's presence. His face showed no signs of wrinkles, or age, but the stranger appeared to carry himself as a man in his mid- to late-thirties.

His hair was black, and his face was clean-shaven; he was somewhat handsome. He seemed to be a person made to be forgotten the moment he was out of sight. Everything about him was ordinary. A man meant for a mediocre life of 9-5, and pointless conversations around a water cooler in attempts to avoid the meaningless paper pushing that had become the way he defined his life. Everything about him seemed average. Well, almost everything. His eyes told a different story. They were the most astonishing blend of orange, hazel, yellow, and blue. They told of a secret greatness locked away that offered protection and comfort to whoever sought it. In fact, the stranger's eyes were only slightly duller and less brilliant then his own.

"Hello, Michael."

"Uh . . . hello," Michael said, still staring at the stranger and his odd smile. He had no idea what to say, let alone how this person knew his name. To buy himself some time, he began to reorganize his things on the table. He picked up his book and set it neatly near the end of the table and moved the cup of coffee to a napkin. While doing this he studied the wooden surface of the table in hopes that it could give him some answers, glancing up every now and again. He found no answers. Finally, he looked up at the stranger, who still sat with a complacent smile, and asked, "Do I know you?"

The stranger thought of the best possible answer he could give that would be both the truth and not too confusing to understand. "Yes and no. You know me, but you don't remember me."

"Where do I know you from?"

"From your past."

"What's your name?"

"My name is Sebastian, but you can just call me Bastian."

Michael laughed to himself. He had always loved the name Sebastian, but never knew of anyone who actually had the name, besides in the movies. So he knew that he did not know this stranger; he must have mistaken him for someone else. Yet, how did he know his name?

"How do you know my name?" Michael asked.

"I've known your name for a very long time, but that's beside the point. What matters is that you told me to meet you here, in this coffee shop, at this table, at this hour, at this minute. You told me to come on this date to see if you were ready."

Both sat quietly for a moment. Bastian asked, "Well . . . are you?"

"Am I what?"

"Ready?"

"Ready for what?"

"To leave."

"And go where."

"Home."

In any other situation, Michael would have been worried, weirded out, and frustrated by the presence of a stranger he had never met, who knew his name, and was asking if he's ready to go home. But for some reason, he wasn't. This strange man who called himself Sebastian did not seem threatening in the least. Michael knew that he wasn't dangerous. He couldn't explain it; he just knew. There was truth in his voice and in his eyes that told Michael to listen and not worry.

"When did I tell you all this?"

"Twenty-three years ago."

"That's impossible. I'm twenty-three years old."

"I know," Bastian said with a reassuring smile.

Michael sat back in his chair and stared in confusion. This was ridiculous! How could he have told him to meet him here, at this café, at this table, at this exact time, before he was even born? Was he supposed to understand, or was he justified in his confusion? He decided not to ask and to wait for Bastian to speak again.

The jazz music continued to play overhead, and the sound of a nearby conversation could be scarcely heard. Still, Michael waited for Bastian to speak. Seconds ticked away and, just when Michael was close to his breaking point, Sebastian said something unbelievable.

"I'm an angel."

"What does that mean?"

"It means that I am an angel."

"Like a real angel? With wings?"

"Yes."

"From heaven?"

"Yes."

With each passing word Michael became more convinced that this stranger was a lunatic no matter what his eyes seemed to say about him. Michael was the one smiling now, sarcastically. If Sebastian was insane, then there was no harm in having a little fun.

"So you mean to tell me that underneath that coat of yours are wings—wings with feathers that you use to fly?"

"Yes." Bastian never stopped smiling.

"Wow! This is too funny! Who put you up to this—Kevin, Adam, who?"

"You did. You told me to meet you here, at this exact time, dressed as the person you see before you, to see if you were ready."

Michael continued to smile, but now he was beginning to feel a little uneasy. There was no way he was telling the truth. Angels didn't really exist . . . did they? What if he was an angel and he was telling the truth? What would it mean? If this 'angel' was telling the truth, then it could mean only one thing. The smile left Michael's face as he sat forward in his seat and looked at Sebastian. He asked with a serious expression, "Am I dead?"

Bastian burst into laughter. "No, no, you are very much alive."

"Did you come here to kill me?"

"I could never kill you."

"Am I going to die soon?"

"You can never die."

"Okay, this is starting to get weird. Who are you?"

"I told you my name is Sebastian."

"Are you the Grim Reaper, here to collect my soul?"

"No, I am not the Grim Reaper."

"I'm not playing anymore." Michael was becoming agitated. "Why are you here and how do you know my name? Truthfully! No jokes and no confusing answers!"

The smile finally faded from Bastian's face. He adjusted himself in his seat, leaned forward, rested his arms on the table, looked Michael in the eyes, and began to speak.

"Twenty-three years ago, you told me to meet you here and ask you if you were ready to come home, or to live out the rest of your life as you have been. You said that you would have an answer by now. You also told me to tell you the truth about why you were here and the reason for your existence in this form."

"The reason for my existence?"

"Yes. You said that by this age your human mind would be able to handle the truth about what you truly are."

"Which is what?"

Sebastian breathed in deeply and let out a long sigh before he spoke.

"You, Michael, are not human. It is true that you were born, and you have human parents, but that was all planned. You wanted to become human in order to understand how people were changing, if they were changing at all—the way they were thinking, the way they felt, the reason they seemed to be moving so rapidly, and whether others still knew and felt your existence. You wanted to understand the thoughts of people, so you figured the best way was to become a person yourself. You wiped out the memory of who you are and allowed yourself to be born to human parents—to be raised as a child who would one day grow up to become a man. You didn't want to be told of people's hardships by an outside source any more, or to view it from far away. You wanted to actually experience it—to feel the good emotions along with the bad and be able to relate to the way humans are today. People had changed so much since their first steps on this earth, and somewhere along the line you felt as if you had lost touch with them. The only way to regain that connection is to walk among them and know their thoughts as your own. You don't remember who you are, what you created, and the true strength of your abilities, but deep down you are very special. You are more than human. You are more important than any being that has ever and will ever exist in all of time. You, Michael . . . are God."

With these last words, Sebastian looked into Michael's eyes. They stared at the other across the table. Sebastian waited for his words to sink in, while Michael hoped the smile would reappear on the stranger's face. Neither happened.

"You're kidding right?" Michael exclaimed. Sebastian said nothing, but continued to stare into Michael's eyes until finally he spoke.

"I believe you have done this before."

"What? You mean become human?"

"Yes."

"How many times?"

"That, I do not know. No one does, except you."

"How is that possible?"

"What isn't possible? You have the power to control all of existence. No one knows the full range of your powers, if they have a limitation, but you. You have the ability to rewind time, alter the future, or change someone's fate. You know no bounds and so live by the rules you create."

This was too much to handle. What did this mean? What was the point to any of it?

"So what are you, some kind of messenger-angel or something?" Michael said jokingly.

"Delivering this message is only part of my job. The other part is to watch over you every day, all day. I've been with you since the day you were born and will be with you until the day you die. I'm your guardian."

The smile faded from Michael's face. "This is insane! This makes no sense at all. You mean to tell me that I am God? All powerful, all knowing, almighty God, and you have been watching over me since the day I was born? Okay, then what's the name of my sister?"

"Michelle."

"What about my brother?"

"Kevin."

"What is the name of my dead dog?"

"You never had a dog."

"Anyone could know that stuff." Michael tried to think but couldn't. "This is bullshit! If you're an angel, and you're supposed to know everything about me, then tell me about all the sins I have committed in my lifetime. Explain to me why it is that I am prejudiced against certain people. Why aren't I understanding and patient all the time? I get agitated when I have to stand in a line for more than five seconds for God's sake! You see! I take the Lord's name in vain. I curse. I sure as hell don't go to church. I've had sex. I lie. I've stolen. I've even tried a few drugs. Explain to me what kind of God has done those things. Not this one, because I'm not Him."

"You are Michael. Right now, in that seat, you are Michael. But inside of you lies the soul of God. You carry greatness with you, yet you do not know it. You are learning right from wrong, just as every other person does in this world. No one is without sin. That is why you carry Him with you. So that He can learn and fully understand what it means to be human."

Michael shook his head in disbelief. "No. This is bullshit! I have a family, and friends, and people that I love. I am no God. I am an ordinary guy in his early twenties with his whole life to live. And you come in here and tell me that I'm God. No! There's no way, none."

Michael paused and saw that Sebastian had not been moved by these words.

"All right then, prove it. If I'm God, then why don't I have any special abilities? Why can't I walk on water, or fly, or do a whole bunch of supernatural stuff?"

"You have built up walls that prevent you from using your powers. These walls will only begin to come down when you reach old age and you are much more calm and wise from your years spent here on earth."

This was all wrong. This could not be happening. How could it be? Him? God? No way. It was too much to handle and understand. This wasn't real. It couldn't be. For him to accept it, he needed proof.

"Show me your wings."

"What?"

"If you're an angel, show me your wings. That is the only way I can believe you. The only way I will believe you."

"Here?"

"Yes. Take off your coat and show me. Now."

Bastian looked across at Michael and could tell that this was the only way he could gain his trust. He weighed his options and, after a few seconds, said, "Fine."

The room went silent. The jazz music stopped playing. The people in the restaurant had all stopped moving and talking in mid-sentence. Michael could even see through the glass door that the cars on the street had stopped moving. He looked around and saw that he and Bastian were the only two not affected. And Bastian had stood up and was undoing his shirt.

Michael sat in front of him, not knowing what to expect. As the shirt fell to the carpeted floor, white features appeared over the shoulders of Bastian and on each side of his arms. The wings first appeared small, as if they were too small to carry the weight of a person, or even a child. Then Bastian stretched his back muscles and pushed the tips of his wings as far as they could go. His eyes were closed, and his face showed

115

the expression of a person in deep concentration and even a little pain.

Michael looked at each feather and saw they were perfectly shaped and in amazingly precise order. They were the wings of a hawk or an eagle, enlarged, whitened, and placed on a man. Nothing could compare to their splendor. And Michael would forever only know pure beauty as what he witnessed on that afternoon.

Bastian opened his eyes and saw a tear fall from Michael's eye. The tear fell not only because of the beauty of Bastian, but also because Michael knew he was telling the truth. Everything he said was real. Now, he had to make a choice.

"I'm not here to tell you to come with me. I'm here to see if you are ready—to ask if you think you have seen enough of this world to understand the life you have been given. If you think you have, then come back with me. However, you can choose to stay and live out the rest of your life. The only thing that will change is the truth you now know about your life—everything else will remain the same. I will continue to watch you, but I won't interfere in your life in any way to alter your path. This is yours to live and do with as you wish, whether that be good or bad. The decision is yours."

Michael didn't know what to say or how to think. His mind was a mess and he had no idea what he wanted to do. Should he go or stay?

"Stop."

Michael got up from his living room chair and walked over to the scene that had been taking place before him. Bastian got up as well. Both studied the images of their paused selves stuck in that moment. Before his very eyes, Michael was about to make the biggest decision of his life, to stay on earth and live out the rest of his life as the man he wanted to be. And Bastian was about to vanish from sight. Both knew what was going to happen because it had happened before. This was the past replaying itself. It wasn't supposed to change, but it did.

"I have to tell you something," Michael said.

Bastian looked at the old man Michael had become as he stood next to his younger self.

"This is not as it seems."

"What do you mean?"

"I mean that you were misinformed."

"I don't understand."

Michael breathed out a heavy sigh. "Bastian, the message I told you to send me wasn't correct."

"I still don't understand what you mean."

"Since you arrived at my cabin I have been getting these powers—these abilities to change reality as I saw fit, just as you told me I would. With those powers came a truth. A truth that had been locked away inside of me that could only be revealed with the unleashing of these powers. A truth you put there."

Michael looked into the confused eyes of the angel and told him the secret that no one in all of existence knew until a few hours ago.

"Bastian, I'm not God . . . you are."

Bastian smiled. "No, you are God. I was chosen to watch over you and deliver you the message."

"That's right—you were chosen to watch over me. You watched my entire life, day by day, just as I did. You lived the same life I did, so you saw and learned the same things as well. You sent the message that you had given to yourself. I was there when it happened."

Bastian continued to look confused and intrigued.

"On the day before I was born, plans were changed. I was supposed to watch over you throughout your life, as your guardian, and deliver to you the message that you delivered to me. But we switched roles. You transplanted your soul into my body and I took your place here on earth. The memory of what took place was wiped from our memories. No . . . not really wiped, but moved. Not to be remembered until the day you came to take me back. This is the message I was to give to you when all this was over. The moment I agree to go back with you, you will remember and things will return to normal."

Bastian shook his head. "But why? Why not continue with the way things were originally planned?"

"Because it is as you said—God goes by his own rules, but he is not without compassion. Allowing me to live out a human life from birth to death, while watching me every day, gave you enough of the information you needed. Unfortunately, to remain objective in your views, the lie had to continue, with you delivering to me the message that I am God and continuing to think you are only an angel."

It all made very little sense, and Bastian had no idea what to do next.

"So you are me, and I am you."

"Yes."

Bastian looked down at the ground and calculated what this meant. Inside of him lay the soul of the most powerful being that ever existed and will ever exist. And yet he felt afraid at what it all meant. He did not want this responsibility or this power. It was too much for him to understand, so he asked for help.

"What do we do now?"

"Now, we go home."

Bastian nodded his head in agreement.

"Can I tell you something?" Bastian asked, looking over at Michael as they headed towards the front door. "I'm afraid."

Michael stopped walking and looked over into Bastian's eyes. "Now, you know. Now, you know what it means to be human. Nothing is certain for people, nothing makes sense, the right decision is never clear. But even though the fear of making the wrong choices stays throughout a person's life, he keeps going. He never gives up. He hopes that he is making the right choices and has faith that tomorrow will hold something better than today. He hopes."

Their eyes were locked together. At that moment, they were no longer angel and God; they were both human and knew what it meant to be human. They had lived a full life, and they took every lesson they learned with them. They looked away from one another and out the glass door of the coffee shop. There were no cars, no people; there wasn't even a street. All that existed was light, golden and white. Outside those doors lay an existence they would both view with different eyes. Michael reached for the handle and pulled the door open as they walked out together.

As the door closed behind them, time resumed for Bastian and a much younger Michael. With his wings extended to their full length in the coffee shop, and Michael looking up into his eyes, he asked, "Have you made a choice?"

Be

There are repercussions to being the victim, as a child, of sexual assault and an unstable household. One of them is that every eight to ten years I get an allergic reaction to living and, in an attempt to self-medicate, go crazy. So far, this has happened three times. The first was during my senior year in high school. At the time, I didn't believe it had anything to do with being rapped when I was eight years old. There were so many other domestic problems, it was hard to keep them all straight.

While my friends were all worried about playing in the "big game" on Saturday, who they were going to take to prom, and whether or not the girl in freshman biology really, maybe, possibly, hopefully liked you a little bit to let you feel on her booty during a slow dance; so was I. The only problem was, I also had the problem of figuring out whether or not I was going to get any sleep that night because of the trivial arguments my parents would have during the night. By my senior year, the question had evolved from *would I get any sleep in my own bed in my own house* to *where were my mother and me going to sleep for the night.*

During my junior year in high school, my parents separated. I came home from cross-country practice—thrilled to be good at a sport that didn't require the co-ordination of bouncing, catching, or throwing a ball of any sort—to my mom telling me to pack my things. I can't say I was surprised. My parents had been arguing since before I was born. They were separated before I was born, but I was the uniting factor that brought them back together. Their arguing had even caused my brother Daniel to move out in his senior year of high school when Daniel and Dad got into a fist fight, as described in the novella *Michael*. Seeing Daniel (who weighed 150 pounds) lift my father (who was close, if not over, 250 pounds) by the throat, while hearing my sister and Mom scream for Daniel not to kill my father, is a memory I will never forget.

Most days, my mother would dread my father coming home. Shortly before my parents' separation, my dad had been made redundant by Multi-Ad Services, a computer and advertising agency. They were laying off workers and my dad had called off too many days to stay home and pick arguments with Mom when she had the day off from Kmart. He spent days and nights drinking too much and arguing whenever possible.

Mom had taken to hanging out with her cousin Cheryl, getting her hair done into finger waves instead of the all-natural look she had been sporting since the late eighties, and playing the song "Hold On" by Sounds of Blackness on repeat. All these things he despised, and he let her know whenever he could. Although they had been arguing since the day I was born, I did notice that things had taken a dramatic turn for the worse.

Weeks before they separated, I came home to find the kitchen floor covered in cooking oil. My father was sitting at the kitchen table smoking a cigarette, staring off into space while sipping a beer. All he said as I walked through the door was, "Your mom went down to Cheryl's so you're going to have to find yourself something to eat."

I was under the impression that he had been trying to fry himself chicken (very unsuccessfully) spilled the cooking oil, felt disheartened over his failure, and sat down to drown his sorrows in a cigarette and beer. What had actually happened was he and my mother had gotten into yet another argument about who knows or cares what while she was frying chicken. One thing led to another. Yelling ensued. And rather than walk away and calm down like a civil adult, Mom tried to throw scolding grease on Dad. She missed, and the pan of oil splashed out of the pan in the wrong direction, landing on her instead. The third degree burn left a scar on her chest that she still has to this day.

So, when I came home and she told me to pack, I knew the day had been coming.

I packed, getting clothes for the week, and anything else I might need, having no idea where we were going and when we would be coming back. We packed up the car and drove five minutes to my cousin Cassandra's house. Up until that moment, I had no idea that I had a cousin Cassandra, let alone where she lived. Luckily, it was a two-minute walk from Adam and Jordan's houses—two of my best friends at the time—so it made getting a ride to and from school much easier, while also giving me an excuse to get out of the house when I needed to clear my head. We brought our things inside, settled in the basement, and were told to make ourselves at home.

Home? I thought. *What home? It's a basement.* Granted, it was a nice basement—carpeted and fully finished and furnished, with two side rooms adjacent to the main living room that included a big screen TV and a wraparound couch. The two side rooms included a laundry room, where I kept my computer, and a bedroom with a dresser and a small TV. Like I said, nice, but still a basement.

Most nights, I slept on the couch in the living room. I can't remember sleeping in the same bed as my mom, but I may have slept on the floor. We lived there for about a year while my father stayed in the house, and my parents attempted to work things out in their marriage.

The night my mother and I moved out, my father had no idea where we had gone. She left no note with any indication when, or if, we would return.

I imagine that when neither my mother nor I had returned home by midnight, he knew we weren't coming back. Odds are that he believed we were at Cheryl's. He may have even gone to her apartment, looking for Mom's car, but, seeing we weren't there, driven home and waited until morning. Then he knew he could find out where we had gone because, since the fifth grade, I had been waking up at 4 a.m. to deliver newspapers for the Journal Star. And, since the fifth grade, those papers had been dropped off at the corner of Western and University to be picked up and delivered, come rain or shine, 365 days a year, seven days a week. This meant that at 4 a.m., my father knew where to find me and, so, would find out where to find my mother.

I arrived at the corner in my mother's car to see my father sitting, waiting quietly in his car. He got out and asked where we had gone. I said I had to deliver my papers, and he left it at that. Instead of interrogating me, he let me do my job. He knew he only had to wait.

I delivered the papers as my father slowly followed me in the car, moving from house to house, careful to not lose track of where I was. Afterward, I drove to Cassandra's and went inside to get ready for school. Before walking through the door, my father told me to tell Mom to come outside. "Tell her we need to talk," he said. I did. And when I left, they were sitting in his car. I walked to Adam's and waited by his car to go to school. Then and now, I resent my parents for putting me in the middle of their problems.

For an entire year, the nonsense continued. My parents would talk, my father would stay in the house, and my mother and I would stay at Cassandra's. There was never really a question of with whom I would choose to stay. It was not simply because my father intimidated the entire family into submission, forcing us to lock ourselves in our rooms or tiptoe around the house on eggshells, unsure of his mood and whether or not it would swing like a pendulum, releasing his wrath. It also had to do with the fact that she was my mother. She needed help. In my mind, it made sense. If he wouldn't take care of her, then the responsibility landed on me. It's the only reason I never left to stay with friends, coaches, or teachers. There were offers, but I stayed. What else could I do?

It was then that I stopped feeling.

However, while in middle school, high school, and college there was always one location where I felt that I was allowed to be me: the stage. Acting on stage and off was the only true bastion of freedom I was allotted. By my high school graduation, the repertoire of plays I had been part of were: *Hello Dolly*, *Charlie Brown*, *The Ragamuffins*, *Winnie the Pooh*, *The Little Mermaid*, *Cinderella* (x2), *The Best Christmas Pageant Ever* (x2), *Grease, Lil Abner*, and *Guys and Dolls*. Not all of these were these school plays, but others were productions of Peoria's Children Community Theatre. Twice a year, spring and fall, Glen Oaks would publish and distribute through the Journal Star a magazine of all the community events that would be transpiring over the next six months. On those mornings, I would search the table of contents, find the theatre section, and see what production would be available for auditions in the coming months.

Auditions usually entailed singing a song, and I would normally sing "Can't Wait to be King" from *The Lion King*. The song was fun and could be easily recorded from the movie and played in the background as I sang. Eventually, I moved up to "Go the Distance" from *Hercules* or "A Whole New World" from *Aladdin*. I hated auditioning. It was nerve wrecking to be in front of strangers, singing and performing. And I was usually the only black, which made me feel, once again, that I wasn't being black enough.

There were a few things wrong with my auditions. Problem one: my music was never quite like the others. All the other kids had sheet music that they gave to the piano player. I, on the other hand, had my mother's tape recorder with a microphone that I had used to record the songs directly from the videotaped movie we videotaped from the Disney free weekend or dubbed from a movie we rented from Blockbuster. Problem two: during most auditions for Children's Community Theatre, I was there alone while everyone else had their parents along for support. Both my parents worked, or really didn't want to spend part of their Saturday listening to every "hot" Disney song of the time, so most of the time they dropped me off and came back to pick me up. Sometimes I went to work with my mother and walked over to auditions from K-Mart, which was right around the corner from Glen Oak Community Center.

It doesn't seem like much now, but I always felt like I was doing something wrong or didn't have all the information needed to audition. Around me, parents were giving their children instructions about how to sign in or places to go for additional auditions, while I gleaned what information I could from what they were saying.

Once the audition was over, I had another problem: Since I was the only black in an all-white group, I was cast in the chorus and given three or four small parts because they knew I was talented, or given the role of the preacher. In *The Little Mermaid*, they made me dance in every scene because I could do a toe touch. However, occasionally a director would say "fuck it" and give me a leading role. For example, in *Winnie the Pooh* I was cast as Christopher Robin. That role was the most terrifying because at the very beginning of the play, Christopher Robin dances out onto stage, plays with his teddy bear, and then sits in a rocking chair talking to a stuffed bear for five minutes. Did I mention that he's wearing a nightshirt that is really short and for the most part see-through? And, in my first production of *The Best Christmas Pageant Ever*, I was cast as one of the Harolds (the bad kids who run the entire show); all of the other brothers and sisters are white. I guess their mom didn't discriminate based on color if it meant she could get a welfare check.

Needless to say, all of this acting made my father begin to question the manhood of his son. He saw a preteen boy asking to wear tights, ballet flats, and volunteering to put on makeup (while on stage), and he began to wonder if his son wasn't a little . . . different.

Although I loved acting, I eventually grew to hate being on stage. Being placed consistently, year after year, in roles I knew I was better than, really began to get to me. I knew it was simply because I was black and the rest of the cast was white. What was the director going to do besides put the weird black kid in the chorus and hope no one notices? School plays were a little different because the cast was much more diverse, but honestly, I just wanted to act. I didn't want to sing *every single time* the plot started to get interesting. And why was everyone dancing a box step in unison. It didn't make any sense. All the costumes, set building, and preparation for a total of three, maybe four shows. It seemed like a lot of work for very little payoff. It's for this reason that I fell in love with forensics.

By *forensics*, I don't mean C.S.I., but forensics speech and debate. You know, the dorky kids who voluntarily get up Saturday mornings to sit in school classrooms, rehearse in front of blank walls, and perform memorized scripts to an audience of six or seven people. It may not sound like much to you, but these people, these Saturdays, completed me. In college, forensics was my life. It's where I met and fell in love with Sarah. It absorbed every moment of my time and eventually led to me winning state, national, and international tournaments. No one knew, but it was the only opportunity I had to not be the person I hated for as long as I could remember. Without my coach, Paul, and the speech and debate team, I wouldn't have made it through college. I know it's not much, but thank you Leah, Jason, Tony, J. Cole, Ian, Kent, and Michele for letting me be me. Words cannot describe what it meant. This was college. High school offered different family, friends, and sanctuaries to run to when life became too difficult to handle.

The Incident (Fiction)

"Junior, put on your shoes. We're going over to the house to talk with your dad." The teenage boy nodded and looked for his shoes.

What he wore was nothing out of the ordinary: a pair of khakis and a green Tommy Hilfiger button-up shirt, with a short-sleeve white T-shirt underneath. He knew the outfit should be worn with a pair of Steve Maddens, maroon with tan stripes, but still he chose his running shoes. It didn't look right, but still he put them on, unsure why, but knowing he should.

They got into the car, he and his mother.

They drove to their house at North Wilson Drive, parking in the driveway, as they had always done, behind his father's Cadillac.

They entered through the back door, and his father sat at the kitchen table. He stood when they entered.

They all sat.

Parents talked. Junior, the teenage boy, said nothing. He wasn't even listening to what they were saying. Staring into space, he was lost in his own thoughts until, finally, his mother asked, "Junior, what do you think?"

He looked up, and both pairs of eyes were on him. He froze, unsure of what to say, or even what the question had been.

"Junior?"

He looked back and forth from one face to the other. Tears wet his father's cheeks while his mother's eyes remained calm, dry, steady, and unmoved. How did he get there? What was the question?

Rather than respond, he stood up from the table, walked out the back door, and began to run as his parents sat, silent, refusing to call his name.

North Wilson Drive passed in a blur as he moved through side streets, making his way toward Sterling. The sound of rubber soles against wet pavement filled his ears as he took off the green button up and tied the shirt around his waist. The white T-shirt stuck to his skin. He turned onto Sterling, running past headlights along the busy street, letting his feet take him where they wanted.

Eventually, exhausted and tired, they stopped outside his friend Pat's house. Covered in sweat and rain, with khakis glued to his legs, he rang the doorbell. Pat's mother answered the door. Without saying a word, she knew something was wrong.

"Hi," Junior said through gasps of breath, "is Pat home?" Air forced its way in and out of his lungs to his tired muscles. She smiled and nodded.

"Yeah. Come on in, Junior," she said. "Pat," she called, "Junior's here to see you."

He entered with his usual greeting.

"Hey, man. What's up?"

Junior shook his head from side to side, saying, "Nothing. Do you mind if I stay here for a while? Things are kind of crazy at home right now." Tears began to well up in his eyes.

"Yeah, sure man. Of course."

Without asking if it was okay, simply knowing it would be, Pat and Junior moved to the basement. Junior sat quietly. They gave him a towel and maybe some clothes, but he can't be sure anymore. The memory hurts too much to grasp the full details of where he slept, who told his parents where he was, or what eventually happened afterward. All he knows for sure is that it hurt at the time, forcing him to go numb, and, for some reason, just like that night, he felt he needed to go for a run.

The Problem

Eventually, my father left. He moved south to be closer to family. In Peoria, he had no job and no family of his own, so he returned to a safe place to start over. My mother stayed. While working at Kmart full time, she used what little money she had saved, and some she had borrowed from aunts and uncles, to move back into our house on North Wilson. Drive. After paying the money to turn on the lights and utilities the summer before my senior year, the bank foreclosed on our house, leaving me and my mother homeless for the second time in our lives.

I remember the day we received the letter from the bank. My mom sat in the living room on the floor. It was the first time I had ever seen her cry. It was crying that said she had no more to give—no more answers. It was pure hopelessness.

I went over to where she was crouched on the floor.

"They're taking the house," she said through tears. "I was so stupid! I thought your dad had been paying the bills, but he wasn't. I spent all the money getting everything turned back on. Now we don't have anything. What are we going to do?"

All she could do was cry. And all I could do was hold her. I told her what she used to say to me when it felt like my world had come to end, and what she told me when I wanted to commit suicide: everything is going to be all right.

The words felt hollow and weightless, but it was all I could think to say. It was all I could do.

The entire time I held her, I kept thinking, *I can fix this*. I had to be a man. Forget being black, or acting black, or thinking I wasn't black enough. I had to find some way to fix this problem because that's what men do. They provide, nurture, and support. That's what my mom needed and those have been my thoughts ever since that moment (even against the wishes of my therapist).

From the living room I went to the paper, looked up the local rentals, and searched for apartments. I had no idea what I was doing. I saw the words studio apartment and thought of an apartment combined with or above an art or dance studio. I figured I could use the money from my paper route to rent an apartment, but it was a decision I had no say in. Instead, we moved into the basement of my Aunt Tonell and Uncle James.

As I entered my senior year of high school, I began to go crazy.

Most people would expect, given my circumstances and situation, that I would have failed all my classes, fallen apart, and become distant from my friends, coaches, and teachers. But it was just the opposite.

This was my daily schedule:

4:30 a.m.-6:30 a.m. – **Deliver Newspapers** (My three paper routes earned me $100 a week. This money was spent on lunch, clothes, college application fees, graduation fees, and prom, as well as being extra money for Mom, if needed.)

7:15 a.m.-3:15 p.m. – **School** (Classes: AP English, AP Calculus, Honors French, Concert Band)

3:15 p.m.-7:00 p.m. – **Extra Curricular Activities** (Cross-Country, Speech, Track, Theatre, Key Club, Student Council, National Honors Society)

7:00 p.m.-12:00 a.m. – **Work** (Peoria Symphony Orchestra), **Dinner**, **Homework**

12:00 a.m.-4:00 a.m. – **Sleep**

4:30 a.m. – **Start over again**

At the time, I couldn't stay home because there was no home. I stayed busy in order to not think about the cramped basement I lived in that often flooded septic water in the middle of the night or the roaches that crawled over me while I slept. In one cramped corner, I kept a daybed, desk, and the books I owned and loved to drown myself inside. Staying busy was the only way to stay sane. And it worked, most of the time. Unfortunately, there was only so much I could take before eventually breaking. And the one time I did while in high school, I wrote about the incident in my journal.

***

I almost had a breakdown the other day.

I don't have any idea about that happened. Everything that was wrong in my life, the fact that I'm in a place that I have any choice to be in, stress of leaving for college. Everything! Just made me seem as if I was going to go crazy if I spent one more night in this house. So when I thought that I was going to just burst I decided to get a hotel before I hurt myself or someone else.

I called my mom and told her I was going to get a hotel room for the night because I couldn't take it anymore. I tried to explain to her all of the thoughts that were ricocheting off the walls of my brain and all of the anger that was bubbling just below my skin. But I couldn't. She wanted me to talk to her, but I never could and I never can and I never will. Probably because we have too much between us. Maybe her and Daddy hurt me too much. Maybe.

I hung up the phone and packed clothes as if I had very few moments before the house burned to the ground and I had to grab my most valuable possessions. The look in my eyes probably would have scared most people who saw me at that moment. It felt as if I had killed someone and my hands shook with the same fierceness. It scared me to think that I had finally gone crazy and there was no way of going back to the old Junior. I felt that way once before, but it was about three years ago towards my father. That episode passed and so did this one.

I walked out of the room with so much determination you would either think I was late for an appointment, or fleeing a crime scene. I reached the living room and was on my way out, but not before being talked to by Uncle J and introduced to a man that I could have cared less about. I hid my insanity, not well, but hid and was formal enough to be let go out of my cage. However, just when I believed I was home free I was stopped by his son in the car who noticed me from the Omega Psi Phi talent show. I wanted to scream! I said hi and bye as quickly as possible and fled to my red savior of a truck. It was amazing that I could still be polite when I was on the brink of madness.

The key finally reached the ignition and I was a heartbeat away from checking into a hotel for the night, and from running off the road. My hand kept shaking and my mind kept wandering.

I drive to Hamilton Suites, the one I got for prom night. Nothing happened, promise. Although, I do wish something would have, but should a', could a', would a'. I figured they would give me one because they had the last time. I pull into a parking spot and see that my truck sticks out like a sore thumb in that parking lot. The dingy, red, beat up old trunk filled with soda cans and a spare tire in the back didn't exactly match the Expeditions, and Galants, but I was determined to act confident.

I stroll in very nonchalant and asked if there were any rooms available. She replies yes and I proceed to ask for one. The desk clerk said the rooms were about $99, but I was expecting this and showed no signs of disapproval. Money was the last thing on my mind, until she mentioned it, and it quickly became a reality. But, oh well, money is money. She asked if I was twenty-one and I replied that I was eighteen. She gave me a sad look, looked down at her computer for a few seconds, then looked up at me and asked if I was from the area. I said yes, and because of that I couldn't get a room. She said that if I was traveling that it would be a different story. Which made sense to me. So I accepted her decline and thanked her for her time, all the while feeling shattered inside. If my dad was in that situation he would have made an ass of himself and asked to see the manager with that horrible grimace on his face that clearly showed the face of a man who believed he was being wronged because of the color of his skin, rather than policy. I always hate it when people do that because most of the time they are wrong and make an ass of themselves.

So, with no more determination, and an extremely heavy heart I walked out of the sliding doors, to the truck, and drove away. I thought of trying another hotel, but I don't think I could have handled another disappointment. And the money for a room was still a reality in my mind. So I drove. Not around town, but just back to my cell. I could feel my brain returning, but I could also feel the anger brewing just below the surface of my skin. My hands were still shaking but I returned back to J's house and proceeded very slowly to the front door. The quicksand that was spread throughout that area made my feet sink with each step. The dungeon was my only solitude. I stripped off my clothes, left my room a mess from when I left, turned out the lights, and curled up in bed facing the wall with no hope that the 20th would come to deliver me from this life that has been demolished by careless parents. The only comfort was the cover that protected me from the outside world and the warmth from the flesh on my knees touching my chest.

I just laid there. Not thinking, not moving, not sleeping, not even listening to John Mayer playing on my computer. Once again there was nothing, only me. Sometime during the night the phone rang and it was for me. My cousin tried to wake me, but I just laid there pretending to be asleep, or dead. Whichever came first.

***

Eventually, that night and the summer passed. August 20 came, and I left for college at Bowling Green State University in Ohio where I was accepted with full tuition and of the out of state fee fully paid for. Along with numerous other scholarships from my Peoria High School, Omega Psi Phi, and the Journal Star newspaper, my first year of college (including books, room, and board) was completely paid for. Life was great! At least, that's what it seemed to everyone. Just below the surface, beneath the smile, I was on the verge of breaking down completely, until I finally did at the beginning of my freshman year in college.

I lasted one week at Bowling Green—one full week before withdrawing from all my classes, losing all my scholarships, and dropping out.

I lasted only one week at Bowling Green because in high school I thought about nothing, only doing what I needed to do to get out of James and Tonell's basement to live on my own. The only way out I knew was college, so I took every opportunity to ensure I made it, while keeping my mind preoccupied long enough to avoid thinking about how frustrated and depressed I truly was. Any extracurricular I could be a part of, any essay I could write that would lead to another scholarship and away from the life I had been forced to live for too long, I did it. I put every ounce of energy I had into getting to college, and after I did it, I had nothing left. My brain and body were spent. The moment I stepped into my dorm and told my mother good-bye, everything I had refused to feel came rushing in like water over a collapsed dam, and there was no way I could stop the flood.

There was a terrible pain in the pit of my stomach, making it impossible to eat, sleep, and get out of bed. For seven days, I cried, curled in a ball, knees clenched to my chest, struggling desperately for the strength to make it to class, but finding only paralyzing fear, sadness, and anxiety. I was lost, with no idea of what to do, or even what was happening. I asked myself every minute, *What's wrong with me? Why am I acting like this? Why can't I just be normal?* Not once did being raped ten years prior enter my mind. I thought I was over it. I had survived. I could move on. Everything would be fine. This is what I thought. I couldn't have been more wrong.

Finally, after talking with counselors and my mom, I came to the conclusion that I should withdraw from classes, and I did. Immediately, I felt like a failure because both Daniel and my sister had dropped out of college, and I had vowed that wasn't going to be me. It felt like my mom, dad, aunts, uncles, and grandparents were expecting me to be the Great Black Hope. I would be the one to succeed where they had failed. So, to fall short in a fraction of the time each had spent in college was devastating. I thought I had let them all down, and, for the first time since I could remember, I felt normal. I felt like everyone else. I'm sorry to say it, but I felt black, truly black, for the first time in my life, and I wasn't bouncing a basketball between my legs or acting cool. It seemed I could identify, finally, with black culture because I saw myself the way the world sees people of color: worthless, lazy, and unable to live up to their potential. I wanted to be one of the exceptions. I wanted to be one of the few that made it against the odds, pulling myself up by my own bootstraps. But it turned out, I was just like all the others. So much for being unique.

And this, ladies and gentlemen, is the problem. No one told me (no one *still* has told me) that this kind of thinking is wrong. Being black doesn't mean you're a failure. It shouldn't mean the odds are forever *not* in your favor. What it should mean, however, is that because life is hard, you're better suited to survive life's challenges. Unfortunately, it doesn't mean that either.

I'm a teacher in inner-city Baltimore, where over 70 percent of the students live in poverty, and 99.9 percent of them are black or of color. I have taught grades six through ten, and every year, month, and day, I see students who are living the life I lived. They have one parent or no parents. They're homeless and have no definite idea where they're going to lay their head at night, let alone who's going to be giving them their next meal. Their families have little money for school uniforms or a $5 book we ask them to purchase for class. They come to school sleepy, unclean, and under-educated. The only difference between them and me at their age is that they think and believe, beyond a shadow of doubt, that this is all there is. The way their parents live is how it will always be because they know no one who has done otherwise. I saw education as my only escape because I couldn't play basketball or football. My asthma, and not being able to afford medication, kept me from running or thinking of track or a cross-country scholarship. However, my students see sports as their only option because the only individuals they've seen make it out have done so through sports (or rapping). The rappers and sports players are their models for success and no one has told them this model of supposed success fails more times than it succeeds. What they have seen firsthand from the large majority of middle class white teachers who enter the profession for two years, think they've done their civil duty, and head off to law or medical school (yes, I am talking about Teach For America) is that education leads to a dead end. It's impossible. They think I'll never succeed. They also believe: If I do succeed, so what? What's it good for? As long as I pass, that's all that matters. From what they have seen, and *not* been told, scholarships for blacks only come from basketball or football. Academic scholarships don't exist because who do they know that has navigated the system down that path, let alone made it *through* college? They don't have the dreams I had while watching *Full House* and *Step-By-Step*. They don't see the happy, smiling, white faces living in clean houses without bill collectors calling and having little worry that the lights or water or heat would be turned off. I wanted that life. I didn't want arguments. But they don't see it, except when they see me.

When my students see me, they can see a black male teacher who cares, teaches, holds them to expectations, holds them accountable, is someone they can relate to, and mentions his wife and kids rather than going to the club or a baby momma. They can see a black make who has graduated with a bachelor's degree and a master's degree from the best school of education in the nation because they deserve the best education, and so do I; they see, for just a moment, the possibilities. But most of the time, they see me as I saw myself, as I still see myself—an anomaly that can't be replicated, as someone unique and different, who goes against the system. I'm impossibility, and that is the problem.

Acknowledgments

I write about the power of trying, because I want to be okay with failing. I write about generosity because I battle selfishness. I write about joy because I know sorrow. I write about faith because I almost lost mine, and I know what it is to be broken and in need of redemption. I write about gratitude because I am thankful – for all of it. – Kristen Armstrong

Friends. How Many of Us Have Them?

I want to thank all the friends, teachers, and coaches who got me through some really tough times. Even if you didn't know it, you kept me breathing and looking forward to another day. Without you, I wouldn't be here. You were my family, and I love all of you for that.

First, my wife, Sarah—since we were friends in college, you've always stuck up for me and been there to keep me strong when it seemed no one else could or would. You were my best friend for three years, my roommate when I moved in with you and your fiancé, my lover after you accidently fell down the steps on your way to forensics complex and our cheeks touched long enough to change both our lives, and the mother of my children. You've held me through the nights and early mornings when I couldn't stop shaking from fear and anxiety. You sat by my side when I told doctors all the thoughts going through my head, and you never once judged me. You've supported and encouraged me throughout this entire process, and I couldn't have asked for a better cheerleader. I love the life we've built together; I couldn't imagine it being with anyone else. Thank you. Thank you. Thank you.

In middle school, when my parents were arguing every other night, and I was going through the normal seventh and eighth grade losing of the mind due to raging hormones, I couldn't have made it through without my best friends Leila,

Lindsay, Marcus, Shannon, and Jessica. That Nickelodeon alarm clock you all chipped in and bought for my birthday is among the top three gifts I've ever received. And I still have the card and all the notes we passed back and forth between classes. I look back at them every few years to remind myself of the good friends I had.

In high school, cross-country was my life. Everyone on the team was family. The Buddies: Pat, Bryan, and Adam. Remember the beats we would make up on the spot; the dog pile we would make with the girls' team pretty much as an excuse to be close to Ally and Holly still makes me smile. Thanks for coming to try and find me when you thought the note I had written was a suicide note. The CD player the team bought me to replace the one that was stolen from my locker is among my top three gifts as well.

Jordan, the drives we would take were invaluable. Just hanging out at your house, playing poker in the cul-de-sac or your basement late at night, playing video games, or talking about life while you smoked, got me through a lot of tough days and nights when I didn't want to go home because I didn't have a home to go to.

Coach Phoels, Coach Lawless, Mrs. Burroughs, Mrs. Litterist, and Paul, you were not only my teachers and coaches, but my parents. There's so much I could write here about what each of you meant to me, but just know I wouldn't be alive to write this if all of you hadn't been a major part of my life.

Sully, thanks for picking up the phone and having no problem driving me to the emergency room when I had thoughts of committing suicide. You're a true friend, buddy. I may not be here if you hadn't picked up.

Susan, thanks for making me healthy. Without your help, I never would have had the strength or the courage to write any of this.

And last, but definitely not least, Adam. You were my best friend in elementary school. You introduced me to two of the five greatest loves of my life: grape juice and sugar cookies. We lost touch in middle school when you went to the "smart school" and I went to Sterling Middle School, but we picked up right where we left off when we got to Central. We worked together setting up chairs for the Peoria Symphony Orchestra; shared bowls of beef-fried-rice at Heidi's family restaurant, Ming Shee; and jumped naked into the Illinois River in the middle of November during our last cross-country practice. You still remain my best friend to this day. You were in my wedding, saw both Mirus and Amare before anyone in my family could make it to see them, and you make me laugh on the phone after two seconds. I never told you about being sexually abused, but you were there when I was homeless. You held me together by simply being there, and for that I am eternally grateful. For that I offer you this toast.

Toast (Fiction)

Excuse me. Can I have everyone's attention, please? Hey! Hey! Eyes up here! I'm the best man, and, according to tradition that dates back to the dawn of mankind, you have to listen to me . . . Thank you. Now, there is a format to how these things are supposed to proceed and procedure that must be followed. I know because I looked it up and wrote it down. Hold on a sec as I . . . put on . . . my glasses . . . There! That's better. Forgot the contacts. Now, it says here the first thing I should do is . . . compliment how good the bride and groom look together, tell a memorable story about the bride and *or* groom, connect the story to their loving relationship, and then toast. Seems easy enough.

All right. First things first. Don't they look beautiful together, folks? Part one . . . check. But, honestly, do I really need to say that? I mean look at them. They were made for each other. Mr. and Mrs. Dashal Joseph. I've never seen my best friend so happy, and we've been best friends for a very long time. I introduced him to the two greatest loves in his life, besides Samantha of course—sugar cookies and grape juice. Don't laugh. It's true. Dash, you remember. The last day of school in the fourth grade. It was a half-day, and you came over my house because your mom had to work. We've discussed the sequence of the events of that day many times over the years. The playing of tag on the school jungle gym, the swinging on the swings in the early summer sun, and the playing of the best game in existence, Teenage Mutant Ninja Turtles on the Super Nintendo. It was a great day. However, if you ask Dash, the most memorable part of the day was not the . . . social camaraderie, but the spread my mother offered for lunch. Later tonight ask him to tell you about that meal and it will be as if he is retelling the delicacies of the Last Supper; no offense, Father. In fact, I'll tell you. We ate chips, salsa, sugar cookies, and grape juice. Nothing spectacular to you and me, but to Dash it was a lunch fit for the gods. With one bite of the chips and a dollop of salsa, he proclaimed they had to have been stolen from an authentic Mexican family's cupboards. As the frozen, sliced, and baked sugar cookies entered his mouth, he knew for certain he had been allowed to pass through the gates of heaven and bask in its splendor before returning to earth. And with one sip of the purple grape juice, he lost all sense of who he was, where he was, and how he got there. Apparently, no one told little Dashal that the thimbles of juice that were supposed to represent the blood of Christ could be bought at any local Seven Eleven. He was amazed at the powers my kitchen held and said I was the best friend he ever had. I can still picture his purple-stained lips.

Unfortunately, it wasn't meant to last because that was the final time I saw him for the rest of my pre-pubescent life. Due to circumstances neither of us could control, we went to different middle schools and lost contact. Mostly because we were boys, and the idea of calling another boy on the phone was beyond our realm of understanding. As far as we were concerned, the other had died, fallen off the edge of the planet, gone to space camp where they were recruited to become a full time astronaut to never return, or, most likely, moved out of state. We would not see each other for four years. Our reunion would come with the merging of school district lines to bring us together again in high school.

Freshman year. Cross-country hell week. I had no intention of joining cross-country, Dan. Yeah, we know who you are, put your hand down. Dan was too afraid to go alone, so he asked me to go with him. The only problem was Dan didn't show. He said something about family vacation, nauseating fear, something I can't remember. So, there I was, sitting in the bleachers of Wilson High School, alone, scared, and wondering why the hell I was there. I am so sorry, Father. There are a lot more references to heaven, hell, and the Bible than I realized. I'll try and wrap this up. Anyway, there I was alone and questioning whether or not I should just leave when, all of a sudden, in walks Dash. The best friend I thought I had lost to a vicious and unprovoked shark attack off the coast of Venezuela, or a freak four-square accident that erased his memory and prevented him from remembering my phone number or who I was. Again, these are the thoughts of a fourth grader, or Ryan last night after four Irish car bombs and six beers. Kidding. Kidding. I'm kidding, Ryan! Calm down! We said nothing happened and we meant it. At least . . . never mind. Moving on.

Dash came over, sat down next to me, and didn't say a word. I thought, *Maybe a four-square accident really did take away his memory. Or, maybe he was lobotomized. If only there was some way to remind him of who I am. Some sign I could give him to bring him back.* All of my fears were put to rest when, while out on our first road run, he turned to me and said, "Good job, Jacob," and sprinted off to join the pack of varsity runners, proving why we call him Dash. At that moment, I knew two things: I hated Dan for making me join cross-country, and I had my best friend back.

Of course he did the nerdy speech and debate thing in the winter while I wrestled, like a man. But, every spring and fall, we would be running side by side—or, rather, one far, far ahead of the other. We even ended up getting a job together working for the symphony orchestra—nothing amazing, just setting up and tearing down chairs, but decent money for minimal work. We would skip school, occasionally, to pick up some thick burgers at Hardees, or Chinese food before work, or sugar cookies from the bakery on Prospect. Now that I think about it, our relationship has been based mostly around food— gyros, cheese steaks, gondolas. It couldn't last forever. Eventually, high school ended and Dash went to college in Ohio. He wouldn't come back very often, but we never lost touch. We did eventually learn to call each other. I knew, no matter what was going on, or what new friends I made, Dash would always be there if I needed him. And he knew the same. Each time we talked, Dash would always mention some new girl he was seeing, but he would also mention this new friend of his, Sam. It was always, *Sam this* and *Sam that*. He talked about how Sam was so funny and smart—how they had so much fun while going out for drinks the other night, or preparing some skit for the college speech team. He mentioned Sam so much I started to get a little jealous. This Sam character sounded much cooler and smarter than I did, and that's damn near impossible. So, when he called saying how attractive Sam was, and how he was thinking of dating his new best friend, I thought that maybe being on the speech team for so many years had finally gotten to him. Then I realized Sam was actually short for Samantha and I breathed a sigh of relief.

I may not know Sam as well as I know Dash, but I know Dash is a great best friend. And if friendship and now marriage is a fraction as good as our friendship was and is, you two will be happy beyond belief. You two were made for each other, and I'm happy to be a minor character in the story that is your life. So, if you all would, please, raise your glasses and join me in honoring, introducing, and loving Mr. and Mrs. Dashal Joseph and Samantha Griffin.

The End

My life has been blessed with so many amazing people and stories, it seems that there aren't enough pages on which to write them all. Who knows, maybe they'll make it to print, but this was for me, to get this brick off my chest that had been holding me down and nearly drowning me for so many years. Now, I can breathe a little better and know that everything will really be all right.

Review Requested:
If you loved this book, would you please provide a review at
Amazon.com?
Thank You